SOCIAL ISSUES
FIRSTHAND

Interracial Relationships

Other Books in the Social Issues Firsthand Series:

Interracial Relationships

Bruce Alderman, Book Editor

GREENHAVEN PRESS

An imprint of Thomson Gale, a part of The Thomson Corporation

Detroit • New York • San Francisco • New Haven, Conn. • Waterville, Maine • London

Christine Nasso, *Publisher*
Elizabeth Des Chenes, *Managing Editor*

© 2007 Thomson Gale, a part of The Thomson Corporation.

Thomson and Star logo are trademarks and Gale and Greenhaven Press are registered trademarks used herein under license.

For more information, contact:
Greenhaven Press
27500 Drake Rd.
Farmington Hills, MI 48331-3535
Or you can visit our Internet site at http://www.gale.com

Cover photograph reproduced by permission of Emma Rian/zefa/CORBIS.

LIBRARY OF CONGRESS CATALOGING-IN-PUBLICATION DATA

Interracial relationships / Bruce Alderman, book editor.
p. cm. -- (Social issues firsthand)
Includes bibliographical references and index.
ISBN-13: 978-0-7377-2895-8 (hardcover : alk. paper)
ISBN-10: 0-7377-2895-7 (hardcover : alk. paper)
1. Interracial dating. 2. Interracial marriage. 3. Racially mixed people. 4. Race awareness. 5. Race relations. 6. United States--Race relations. I. I. Alderman, Bruce.
HQ801.8.I68 2007
306.7089'00973--dc22
2006020105

Printed in the United States of America
10 9 8 7 6 5 4 3 2 1

Contents

Foreword

Social issues are often viewed in abstract terms. Pressing challenges such as poverty, homelessness, and addiction are viewed as problems to be defined and solved. Politicians, social scientists, and other experts engage in debates about the extent of the problems, their causes, and how best to remedy them. Often overlooked in these discussions is the human dimension of the issue. Behind every policy debate over poverty, homelessness, and substance abuse, for example, are real people struggling to make ends meet, to survive life on the streets, and to overcome addiction to drugs and alcohol. Their stories are ubiquitous and compelling. They are the stories of everyday people—perhaps your own family members or friends—and yet they rarely influence the debates taking place in state capitols, the national Congress, or the courts.

The disparity between the public debate and private experience of social issues is well illustrated by looking at the topic of poverty. Each year the U.S. Census Bureau establishes a poverty threshold. A household with an income below the threshold is defined as poor, while a household with an income above the threshold is considered able to live on a basic subsistence level. For example, in 2003 a family of two was considered poor if its income was less than $12,015; a family of four was defined as poor if its income was less than $18,810. Based on this system, the bureau estimates that 35.9 million Americans (12.5 percent of the population) lived below the poverty line in 2003, including 12.9 million children below the age of eighteen.

Commentators disagree about what these statistics mean. Social activists insist that the huge number of officially poor Americans translates into human suffering. Even many families that have incomes above the threshold, they maintain, are likely to be struggling to get by. Other commentators insist that the statistics exaggerate the problem of poverty in the United States. Compared to people in developing countries, they point out, most so-called poor families have a high quality of life. As stated by journalist Fidelis Iyebote, "Cars are owned by 70 percent of 'poor' households. . . . Color televisions belong to 97 percent of the 'poor' [and] videocassette recorders belong to nearly 75 percent. . . . Sixty-four percent have microwave ovens, half own a stereo system, and over a quarter possess an automatic dishwasher."

However, this debate over the poverty threshold and what it means is likely irrelevant to a person living in poverty. Simply put, poor people do not need the government to tell them whether they are poor. They can see it in the stack of bills they cannot pay. They are aware of it when they are forced to choose between paying rent or buying food for their children. They become painfully conscious of it when they lose their homes and are forced to live in their cars or on the streets. Indeed, the written stories of poor people define the meaning of poverty more vividly than a government bureaucracy could ever hope to. Narratives composed by the poor describe losing jobs due to injury or mental illness, depict horrific tales of childhood abuse and spousal violence, recount the loss of friends and family members. They evoke the slipping away of social supports and government assistance, the descent into substance abuse and addiction, the harsh realities of life on the streets. These are the perspectives on poverty that are too often omitted from discussions over the extent of the problem and how to solve it.

Greenhaven Press's Social Issues Firsthand series provides a forum for the often-overlooked human perspectives on society's most divisive topics of debate. Each volume focuses on one social issue and presents a collection of ten to sixteen narratives by those who have had personal involvement with the topic. Extra care has been taken to include a diverse range of perspectives. For example, in the volume on adoption, readers will find the stories of birth parents who have made an adoption plan, adoptive parents, and adoptees themselves. After exposure to these varied points of view, the reader will have a clearer understanding that adoption is an intense, emotional experience full of joyous highs and painful lows for all concerned.

The debate surrounding embryonic stem cell research illustrates the moral and ethical pressure that the public brings to bear on the scientific community. However, while nonexperts often criticize scientists for not considering the potential negative impact of their work, ironically the public's reaction against such discoveries can produce harmful results as well. For example, although the outcry against embryonic stem cell research in the United States has resulted in fewer embryos being destroyed, those with Parkinson's, such as actor Michael J. Fox, have argued that prohibiting the development of new stem cell lines ultimately will prevent a timely cure for the disease that is killing Fox and thousands of others.

Each book in the series contains several features that enhance its usefulness, including an in-depth introduction, an annotated table of contents, bibliographies for further research, a list of organizations to contact, and a thorough index. These elements—combined with the poignant voices of people touched by tragedy and triumph—make the Social Issues Firsthand series a valuable resource for research on today's topics of political discussion.

Introduction

Since 1967, when the U.S. Supreme Court ruled bans on interracial cohabitation and marriage unconstitutional, interracial relationships have become increasingly common. According to recent census and survey data, the number of whites, blacks, and Hispanics involved in interracial marriages was ten times greater in 2005 than in the 1960s. Among Asian Americans, 12 percent of the men and 25 percent of the women surveyed in 1996 were marrying non-Asians. And in 2000, partly in response to pressure from grassroots multiracial activists, the U.S. Census Bureau began to allow individuals to select more than one racial category on the census form to reflect the changing nature of the demographics of U.S. society.

In spite of these changes, interracial marriage remains relatively rare compared to same-race unions. In 2002 interracial marriages composed only 2.9 percent of all marriages in the United States, and only 5.7 percent of Americans involved in serious romantic relationships were dating or living with partners of a different race. In a study published in 2005, Cornell University found that while youths were more likely than their elders to be involved in interracial relationships overall, they nevertheless remained relatively secretive about them, apparently fearing the disapproval of their families or their peers. Young women are also reportedly more likely to hide pregnancies resulting from intercourse with a partner of a different race.

The relative infrequency of mixed-race unions and the need for secrecy or discretion described by many who date interracially suggest that while attitudes may be changing, a stigma is still associated with such relationships. Historically, interracial relationships were outlawed as part of an overall social strategy to cement the privilege and superior status of wealthy white landowners in a slave-based economy. But while slaves were set free by the Emancipation Proclamation in 1863, and the antimiscegenation laws enacted or inspired by that society were struck down a little over a century later, racial disparity remains a fact of life in the United States and continues to pose unique challenges to the partners involved in interracial relationships. Not only must they deal with the disapproval of significant segments of society, they often must come to terms with racist stereotypes and patterns of thought that they themselves have inherited from the culture at large. Perhaps it should not be surprising that relatively few individuals to date have chosen to meet these challenges. Multicultural therapists and researchers who have studied these issues in depth over the past several decades indicate that healthy interracial relationships, particularly in a society which is still marked by racial inequity and prejudice, demand the development of self-esteem and a mature sense of racial identity among all parties. Interracial relationships involve all who are affected by them or committed to them in an ongoing process of learning.

Developing Racial Identity

Coming to terms with the reality of racism and developing a sense of identity that is free of unconscious or explicit taints of racist thinking are two tasks that researchers such as Beverly Tatum, Janet E. Helms, and W.E. Cross regard as essential in the development of mature interracial relationships in a society which is divided unequally along racial lines. According to Cross and Helms, blacks (or other minority racial groups) and whites go through roughly parallel stages of racial identity development, as members of each group become aware of, respond to, and (potentially) dismantle racist assumptions and attitudes that may have unconsciously informed their thinking and self-identity.

In a paper on racial identity development among young black women, Beverly Tatum writes, "In the first stage . . . , the African American has absorbed many of the beliefs and values of the dominant white culture, including the notion that 'white is right' and 'Black is wrong.'"[1] The individual, as a minority in a white-dominated setting, will unconsciously conform herself to white expectations and will deny that race plays any role in her relationships with her white friends. Transition to the second stage, according to Cross's model, is typically precipitated in adolescence, when the black or minority youth experiences painful acts of racism or social rejection that wake her up to the prevalence of racist attitudes in society. The remaining stages of black (or other minority) racial identity development, while they do not always unfold in strictly linear fashion, involve conscious identification with black or minority culture, rejection of white values and influence, and eventual development and integration of a strong racial identity, which allows individuals to seek out interracial relationships again from a more secure foundation of self-esteem and racial awareness.

According to Helms's model of white racial identity development, white individuals move through similar stages of unconscious identification with white culture as the norm, to a dawning awareness of white privilege (the unearned advantages that are afforded to whites as the dominant group in society), to eventual acknowledgment of their involvement in the maintenance of a racist social order. As with members of minority groups that become aware of the reality of racism, the white individual may go through a period of conscious, exclusive identification with whites, this time in an effort to deny the painful realizations of the previous stage. Individuals may remain indefinitely at this or any stage, but if they continue to process their experiences, Helms maintains that they will also come to a mature sense of (nonracist) white identity that is able to form healthy relationships across racial lines.

Understanding Motivations for Interracial Relationships

People may enter into interracial relationships for any number of reasons. One way to understand the dynamics of such relationships is through the developmental lenses suggested by Cross and Helms. As these models indicate, individuals involved in interracial relationships may be relatively oblivious to the influence of racist beliefs on their identities or motivations, or they may be quite conscious of racist dynamics without being caught or impelled by them.

In a guidebook for individuals interested in interracial relationships, Kimberly Hohman explores a number of possible motivations for dating or marrying interracially. In some instances a person may choose to date across the color line as an act of rebellion, or because others in his peer group are doing it, or because he regards members of that race as exotic or mysterious (e.g., "Jungle Fever" or "Yellow Fever"). In each case the individual is objectifying members of the other race and is not relating to them on an individual, personal basis. On the other hand, a person may choose to date interracially because she dislikes or is not well-integrated into her own culture; her friends may criticize her for wanting to be better than they are or for wanting lighter-skinned babies. In these instances, as with the previous ones, the individual very likely is motivated by unexamined racist attitudes and beliefs and has a weak racial identity. As Hohman writes, "If you're in a relationship for some of the previously mentioned reasons, there's a good chance you lack self-respect."[2]

Other reasons have also been explored. In his work with mixed-race and multicultural clients, psychotherapist Joel Crohn discovered that many couples involved in interracial relationships actively sought them out, some for the reasons mentioned above but also for others: the need to separate from dysfunctional or controlling families or a desire to marry an individual from a different culture which would complement and balance their own. In these instances as well, the individuals may possibly be acting from a weak sense of self and the idealization of the racial other, which Crohn describes as "the other side of the coin of prejudice."[3] However, these reasons are not necessarily pathological and may be offered just as easily by individuals who have faced their prejudices and fears and have consciously sought out healthy interracial relationships.

While Crohn observes that not many of his interracial clients mentioned love or mutual attraction as the main motivators for their relationships, other researchers—such as Maria P. P. Root, who gathered data on interracial couples outside of the context of psychotherapy—list love, shared vision, and common values as predominant motivations. Some couples attest that not only are they conscious of the impact of racism on themselves and on society, they are working together to counter it as well. Maureen T. Reddy, who is married to an African American man, comments that she and her husband have grown stronger and more intimate through a clear understanding of the enormous pressures that racist society would place upon them, and she describes their marriage as a "racial bridge [that has been] wonderfully freeing and endlessly instructive."[4] For these individuals race is no longer a source of separation but a resource for mutual enrichment.

Future Promise

Although the number of individuals involved in interracial relationships still makes up only a small percentage of the total number of relationships in the United States, the steady increase in mixed marriages over the past several decades suggests that public attitudes are slowly shifting. A 1997 Gallup poll, for instance, found that 61 percent of white Americans approved of interracial marriage, which was up from 48 percent in 1991. If current trends are any indication of what is to come, interracial relationships are likely to become more and more common in the coming decades. Interracial activists anticipate that the increasing prevalence of such relationships will further erode racist attitudes. As long as race continues to be emphasized as an important factor in determining social standing and negotiating interpersonal relationships in the United States, however, individuals will continue to form healthy or unhealthy racial identities. Interracial relationships challenge individuals to examine unconsciously held racist attitudes and beliefs that influence their sense of identity but may also increasingly serve as the crucibles in which mature transracial identities are forged.

Notes

1. Quoted in Judith V. Jordan, ed., *Women's Growth in Diversity*. New York: Guilford, 1997, p. 93.
2. Kimberly Hohman, *The Colors of Love: The Black Person's Guide to Interracial Relationships*. Chicago: Lawrence Hill, 2002, p. 6.
3. Joel Crohn, *Mixed Matches: How to Create Successful Interracial, Interethnic and Interfaith Relationships*. New York: Fawcett, 1995, p. 57.
4. Maureen T. Reddy, *Crossing the Color Line: Race, Parenting, and Culture*. New Brunswick, NJ: Rutgers University Press, 1994, p. 17.

CHAPTER 1

Interracial Friendship

An Interracial Friendship Brought Me Confidence and Joy

Itoro Akpan

Writing as a seventeen-year-old high school student, Itoro Ak-pan, a talented gymnast, reflects on the challenges she faced in her eighth grade year as the only African American in an all-white school. In the narrative that follows, Akpan recounts how the support and guidance of her only white friend helped her to deal with racism and intimidation as she tried out for her middle school's gymnastics team, and ultimately helped her to find confidence and joy in her school life.

"Itoro?"

"What?" I replied, sharply reversing my attention from my biology paper to the cracking voice underneath me.

"Are you trying out tonight for the team?" whispered the mudcolor-eyed, blond girl squinched under my lab table.

"Claudia!" exclaimed the professor from across the room.

Claudia sighed and lifted her short and frail body. Seated, she turned and smiled to me.

Claudia Hart was the only white student who was friends with me while I attended my eighth-grade year at Trickum Middle School. Since my first day, she had created a calm atmosphere for me at my first all-white school. She knew I was an outstanding gymnast who was scared to perform in front of the school because of my color. Claudia persuaded me to be the first African American to join that year's Trickum Tigers Gymnastics Team.

Racist Intimidation

As I quickly slipped into my blue leotard in the locker room, a redheaded girl vigorously pushed against my shoulder. I turned and noticed Crystal McKillian, the most popular girl in school. Haughtily, she stared at me and asked, "You're trying out tonight?"

"Yeah."

She hissed and threw her hands on her hips. "If I were you," she added, "I wouldn't."

"Why?" I asked.

She giggled distinctly and whispered, "Nigger."

Alone, I stood there in astonishment as she trotted away. She called me a nigger. Why? I could only reflect in silence and shudder from anticipation and fear.

An All-White Audience

When all twelve gymnasts entered the gym, a thunder of applause vibrated. Nervously, I glanced through the audience to see if I could find Claudia.

I was called to perform on the balance beam. I rose and smiled toward the audience, and in return they gave me no response. Their white faces watched me as I marched toward the beam. I climbed onto it and started to dance my way down to the opposite end. I managed to bend backward, grab hold of the beam, and swing my body over. After landing, cheers came from around the gym. I smiled and finished the routine with a perfect dismount.

After several performances, Crystal was ahead of me by a few points. I waited meekly for my last performance on the floor exercise. As I approached the floor, the audience cheered. I tapped my foot to the first beats of "YMCA" [a popular disco song by the Village People] and performed a series of somersaults diagonally across the floor. I pranced my way to the end of my routine and added strong tumbling techniques.

I was shocked when my scores beamed from the scoreboard—two points above Crystal's. I was awarded and congratulated by everyone in the gym. Lastly, Claudia and I embraced, both sharing our happy moment in tears.

A Friend Who Made a Difference

Without Claudia's loyal guidance, I would have never shared my athletic talents with the school. Because of our friendship, I have a healthier identity and personality. I have achieved not only a sense of racial equality, but also joyful memories of my last years at Trickum Middle School.

True Friendships Transcend Race

Wen-Shin Lee

At the time he wrote the following essay Wen-Shin Lee was an eighteen-year-old student at Mission San Jose High School in Fremont, California. After spending most of his childhood in Georgia, playing with children from many racial backgrounds, he moved during his eighth grade year to the Bay Area of northern California. There, he was surprised to find that the students in his school segregated themselves into race-based cliques.

In the following narrative Lee describes the development of his relationship with the first person he befriended in California—Enrique, a Mexican American student in his history class. As they got to know each other while working on a project together, they discovered that their fathers, both immigrants who had struggled to overcome poverty and adversity, had a lot in common. Lee and Enrique began to eat lunch together and meet regularly out at the basketball court, becoming fast friends throughout junior high.

I spent most of my childhood in Duluth, Georgia, a suburb not far from Atlanta, a place many of my friends in California refer to as the "Deep South". Being one of only a handful of Asian students in my class, most of my friends growing up were Caucasian, African-American, or Hispanic. At the time, I never felt alienated from my peers. Rather, just like them, I would participate in little league baseball, play with the kids on my block from the afternoon until dusk, and wake up early on Saturday mornings to catch my favorite cartoons. Even so, I knew that there was, in fact, a distinct difference between my friends and me. For one, I spoke Mandarin at

Wen-Shin Lee, "Friendship Without Borders," *Growing Up Asian in America—2004 Winners*, Asian Pacific Fund.Org, February 10, 2004. Reproduced by permission.

home and ate with chopsticks almost every night. Come Sunday my parents would cart my two sisters and me to Chinese school, and in the wintertime I found myself celebrating Chinese New Year, a holiday unbeknownst to most of those I knew. And of course, there was my name, Wen-Shin, or also, Winston, Wenchu, Winsin, and a multitude of mispronunciations that plagued my life every time I met someone new. I found myself in a strange juxtaposition—I did not fit fully the labels of either "Asian" or "American".

Ignoring the Rules of Racism

In this way, growing up Asian in America, for me, meant growing up in an environment that fostered tolerance and understanding for other cultures. Since I myself never felt completely inclusive under one cultural label, I felt myself compelled to understand and respect another's culture—it was, after all, the same understanding and respect that I hoped those around me, both "Asian" and "American", would extend.

Thus, when I moved to Fremont, California in the eighth grade, I found the self-imposed segregation of my junior high school quite unusual. In a school roughly 60% Asian, most Asian students chose to hang out with other Asians, and the same held true for most Caucasians. The concept of choosing my friends, if even subconsciously, by ethnicity was completely foreign in my mind. In Georgia my friendships were forged without any thought towards race. In fact, it had been a virtual impossibility given the demographics of the region I lived in. This being so, the first person I befriended in my new school was a Mexican American, despite the unwritten rules of race-based cliques.

The Seeds of Enduring Friendship

Enrique and I became friends through chance, for the most part. Our U.S. history teacher crossed the paths of our fates when he grouped the two of us together for a project near the beginning of the year. Entering his house for the first time I was awestruck by its size and grandeur. Commenting on it, he chuckled and told me the story of how his father had come to America with twenty dollars and a blanket, and over time managed to become the owner of his own electroplating company, which for obvious reasons, found success in the silicon valley. I told him the story of my own father, who lived in poverty in Taiwan before getting into college and receiving a PhD from Oxford University through sheer force of will. We opened up to each other, in essence, and this small act opened the doorway to friendship. Over the course of our next few project meetings we discussed our hobbies and interests, our pasts and our proposed futures. Eventually, we laughed and joked in class, despite our teachers' ire, and at lunch he would come out to the blacktop where I played basketball everyday. The seeds of an enduring friendship had been planted.

Simultaneously, I befriended several other classmates of mine who had approached me with amiability. They were, for the most part, Asian, and most of them lived in the same neighborhood as I did, as opposed to Enrique, who lived on the other side of the school district. Thus, that summer, I cemented my friendship with these newfound individuals. Nearly every day of the summer I was out and about with them, biking throughout the neighborhood, playing basketball and football, watching movies, or playing video games. By the time high school began, I had thoroughly become part of the crew.

In high school, there was no more basketball at lunch, and I, of course, had my crew to hang out with. But it was utterly impossible for me to abandon Enrique, who had befriended me when I had needed it the most. I was set on breaking the mold established in school—I had grown up as an Asian with predominantly Caucasian and African-American friends, and thus, I saw no reason why Enrique should have any trouble being part of a predominantly Asian crew. I prompted Enrique to sit with us at lunch one day, and introduced him to my Asian friends. It was hard for me to discern their feelings. That is, if they had any reservations about accepting a Mexican as "one of us", I could not tell. My worries about the matter were relieved, however, as the school year went on. Many of my friends began talking to Enrique by themselves in school and via instant messaging online. Friendships were established and strengthened, and as the crew grew more tightly knit, Enrique had become a vital part of it.

A Bond Deepened by Distance

In the middle of my sophomore year, Enrique's family was forced to move to Morgan Hill, a forty-five minute drive away, as a result of the economic downturn. It was this event that served as a crucible for our friendship. No longer an immediately accessible friend at school, it would have been easy to fade out of touch had our friendship been weak. But our friendship only grew stronger. He and I would talk via instant messaging almost every night, discussing his new school, new people he had met, and new problems in our lives. Every few weekends his older brother would take him to Fremont, and we would have the opportunity to hang out for the day. Although we were farther apart than ever before, our faith and trust in each other only increased. I never hesitated to come to him with the personal problems in my life, and he did the same with me. Perhaps what was even more satisfying, however, was that many of my Asian friends had gone through the same process as I had, strengthening their relationships with Enrique in his absence from Fremont. Consequently, when Enrique moved back to Fremont in our senior year, our group of friends became closer than ever.

The Measure of Happiness Is the Quality of One's Relationships

Today, my friendship with Enrique is one of the most enduring and cherished relationships in my life. Had I fallen prey to bias and discrimination when I first met him, I would have never known it. Friendship, as I see it, should be an aspect of life altogether blind to the biases of ethnicity or religion. Growing up Asian in America gave me this perspective—when I was a young child, my friends in Georgia never hesitated to associate with me due to my heritage, and I extended the same respect and understanding to them. It is my personal belief that the true measure of happiness in life is the quality of one's interpersonal relationships. Friendship, thus, is one of the vital aspects of satisfaction in life. I am thankful for my experience as a child growing up Asian in America. For through its lessons, I have been able to bring myself great happiness in the form of true friends.

Biracial Identity, Divided Friendships

Greg Wolley

Greg Wolley is an environmental education manager residing in Portland, Oregon. As the product of an interracial affair in the mid-fifties, a time in which romantic relationships between blacks and whites were widely regarded as shameful, he was given up early for adoption to an African American couple. Growing up with his adoptive parents, he identified strongly with black culture and did not learn of his mixed-race heritage until years later.

In the interview transcript that follows, Wolley describes the course of his interracial friendships from his youth in the San Francisco Bay area, when he was a militant in the black awareness movement of the 1960s, to his later friendships as a professional in a largely white industry. Ironically, he notes that his circle of friends was more racially integrated and open during his youth, at the time he was most strongly identified with black culture. As he has grown and his professional and personal interests have changed, however, he has come to feel more at home when he is with his white friends, doing the things he loves— hiking, kayaking, and working on environmental issues.

Wolley describes several attempts to bring his black and white friends together over the years at parties or on outings, but these efforts have not been successful and his friendships remain divided down racial and cultural lines. He says he is frustrated with this but is happy with who he is and will continue to make friends across the racial spectrum.

In the eighth grade I had two friends that I hung around with: One was Portuguese and one was black. And in the ninth grade, I was kind of going through the black awareness, black power movement. That was a real important time, just learning about black history and growing my hair long. It was kind of scary to my parents because they had gone through all the phases they went through, from colored to Negro, and now we're talking about black, which was supposedly a derogatory term. James Brown had this song, *Say It Loud (I'm Black and I'm Proud)*, and that got on my father's nerves. He was like, "Why do you have to say I'm black and I'm proud, I'm black and I'm proud? Why can't you just be Greg? Why do you have to be black?"

A More Integrated Time

I had Huey Newton [founder of the Black Panther Party] posters in my bedroom with his gun belts and everything, and I was kind of semimilitant, but then at the same time my black friends and I all had white girlfriends. It was kind of a trend—it wasn't making a statement; it wasn't conscious at all. It was just a clique of kids that we fell into at school, and the way the Bay Area is set up, there's the flats and there's the hills. And most of those girls lived in the hills right next to Berkeley, very upper-middle-class. Our neighborhood was middle-class: young middle-class couples with growing kids and two cars and two TVs. It was a pretty average neighborhood, nothing really outstanding about it.

So we had this group, and my friends and I went to parties in the hills and the hill kids went to parties in the flats, and it was a great kind of cultural relations. I sometimes think back about the looks from some of the girls' mothers when we all walked in the house at nine o'clock at night, coming to a party. It was like, "Who's my daughter hanging around with?" But that was a good time, and I feel nostalgic about it because I look at all the tension and segregation on campuses now, even in integrated schools, and I just didn't feel that.

This was ninth and tenth grade. And I didn't know yet that I was actually biracial. I'm not sure when I found that out. I knew I was adopted, but I guess I just assumed both my biological parents were black because my adopted parents were black. And then at some point my mother told me my birth mother had a Swedish background. I thought, "Oh, that's interesting," and that's what I believed until I started searching years later and I got my nonidentifying information [information about birth parents, including general appearance, religion, race, ethnicity, etc.] that said Irish.

Discovering a Racial Faultline

At that point I identified as being black. I was comfortable with that, so I didn't feel that this information was an asset or a detriment. It was just who I was. It wasn't until I started going to college and keying into what my interests were and seeing that there weren't any black students in my classes, and when I started working and doing my career, which is environmental work, there were very few people of color doing things that I was doing. In the social and recreational spinoffs of that, which are backpacking and river rafting and a lot of other things I like to do, again, I wasn't seeing black people.

And now, living in Portland—which is a pretty white city—and still working in natural resources, I have almost no contact with black people on a day-to-day basis, and I haven't made any new black friends since I've been up here. I meet people, but nothing's really come of it. If it wasn't for the black friends I formed when I was in junior high and high school—I have a handful I still feel close with—I maybe wouldn't have any, an uncomfortable thought.

Different Interests

Part of this not having new friends is that I felt like I didn't identify in a lot of ways with the average black guy on the street. In some way, yeah, because we're in this society together. I see the culture through the eyes of a black person or a person of color or a minority person, and that's every day and that's all the time. As far as things in common or conversations, it really varies, but I feel like some things are limited.

When I think about my black friends that I went to college with at UC Berkeley, most of them went into business, or their main focus was how much money they were gonna make when they got out of school. So they went into business school or dentistry or law or whatever, and they're doing well and they're successful and we still have links—we get together and we talk about some common things, we talk about relationships—but I've changed or expanded my values over time with spiritual exploration and doing a lot of environmental work, and that's very, very close to me, I'm very passionate about it. And I reach a dead end real fast if I start bringing those things up.

It's unfair to say that has anything to do with race—it doesn't—but it just so happens that the people I spend a lot of time with around these issues happen to not be black, for the most part. I'm excited and happy when I do find someone black that I click with like that. When that happens, it's bringing more parts of myself together in one place, under one roof. I often feel divided up or compartmentalized.

Divided Friendships

There are friends I have that never meet each other. Once when I was in the Bay Area in the mid-eighties, I tried to bring some old friends and new friends together. So I made up a flyer and I called it "East Meets West" because I was living in Marin County, in the west, but I grew up in the East Bay. I had Marin friends that were white and that I had worked with, and then I have East Bay friends, mostly black. It was just that strongly divided, and that's demographics, really. I did the flyer with the bridges and some Chinese symbols about people meeting together, and I sent those out.

I had this little potluck thing at my house, and people mostly hung out with people they knew. Part of it bombed 'cause the weather wasn't good. I had a table set out on a deck, and then it got cold and we ended up hip to hip on the floor of my little studio apartment, all sitting wedged around, forcing these social graces and passing things around. I didn't see any new friendships strike up because of that.

And then a couple times I tried to put kayak trips together because some friends I worked with had a kayak company. I was trying to get some of my black friends to come out on the water. I thought, "This is great! We can be outdoors and people can meet new people!" And that didn't happen, either. That didn't come off, either. They didn't go. They didn't want to do it. And I don't know how to mend that, so it's been a part of my life to have these friends I do these things with and those friends I do those things with. That's just the nature of friends in general; it's not necessarily racially motivated or intended. But often it seems to fall along those lines, and it makes you wonder, "Well, how much of that do I choose? How much of it am I just resigned to, saying, 'This is how it is'? Or how divided am I within myself and am I trying to, in some way, *keep* things separate?"

Not Quite in Touch with the Black Perspective

Going back and forth in different worlds, I realize how many social differences there are—communication differences, interests—and it helps me understand why there's so much division across the country. It's from isolation; there's so much isolation, and never the twain shall meet. So a lot of information is just not gonna make it into the black community about how to maneuver in certain kinds of circles.

As I got into my career, I was going through this kind of separation from so much black, black, black, and I wouldn't notice it until I'd get with my black friends, and they would be talking black this and black that and I'd go to their house and they'd have these statues from Kenya, and I'd go back to my house and I have stuff from China and India. And I go, "Is there something wrong with me? What's missing here? I don't have my *Ebony* magazine on the coffee table?"

When I get together with black friends, we talk from this black perspective—and sometimes I really identify with it, and sometimes I don't. I have friends who, even though they're educated and doing fairly well financially, they still have this "The Man" sort of attitude: "Oh, yeah, we know they're keeping us down, and we can't do this and the glass ceiling and all that." And that's real, but that's something I've never felt. I've always done whatever I wanted to do: I've gone to schools and gotten into graduate schools that I wanted to go to and I've turned down more jobs than I've accepted. I've lived where I wanted to live. I haven't felt those discriminatory things, so I think attitude has a lot to do with it. . . .

Seeking Integration

My sense of identity started to shift when I met some of my birth mother's other children. That made a big difference, and then so did realizing there is a multiracial movement under foot. I felt like I wanted to integrate all myself and that I wasn't alone in wanting to do that, and so when I realized there were people trying to change legislature and change the census and everything, then I felt more comfortable with it.

Initially I thought: My black friends might think this is strange. "Here he is taking Irish-Celt dancing lessons or he's learning Gaelic language. Oh, God, he's gotten real weird on us here. Who's he think he is? He's not black anymore." But they were okay. I don't know all that they thought, but the reaction I got was, "Hey, he knows more about himself."

Mostly, I feel divided, because when I'm with white friends I feel like I'm being myself, but at the same time, just visually, I know that I look somewhat different and probably am recognized as such. A part of me feels that's okay, that's special, that's unique, and there's nothing wrong with that, and I don't feel any barriers. And then when I'm with blacks, sometimes I feel more like an observer than a participant. I feel like I'm usually recognized as being black, and that's okay, but then I also feel like there's some of me that's being left out as far as how I'm perceived, or there's a whole part of me that isn't there. But then there's this comfort level being around black people or older black women, mother figures. It's very nurturing, and it's very comfortable. I found that older blacks, seniors especially, they're always really proud of a younger black that's successful or that they perceive as being professional or doing well or a role model for younger kids. There's this real pride thing that I like being around.

Finding Harmony Inside and Out

It distresses me that there's so much racial disharmony, and sometimes I wonder if Portland, or even the United States, will be the ultimate place that I live. I know there's ethnic and religious strife all over the world, and it's not something one can hide from, but this country is very peculiar to me, and I often feel like I'm not really of here or from here, so I feel like I need to really check out a lot of other places.

Looking at the big blowup [race riots] that happened in Los Angeles with Rodney King and it's the same thing—people are living in the same conditions as they were in the sixties, but now it's their kids and their kids' kids. I don't feel that the government really represents me in many ways at all; not just racially but about environmental policies, social policies, all of which sort of accentuates my otherness, nationally as well as ethnically.

Despite all these internal quandaries and questions that I've had, I like myself and I'm happy with the way that I deal in the world and the way I deal with people. I've found that just sitting down with someone, the way I sit down with you, that's the best way that I link up with people. I just like making connections with people, and that's how I go through my life. I've had friends all across the spectrum, and that's how I always want to live.

SOCIAL ISSUES
FIRSTHAND

CHAPTER 2

Interracial Romance

Learning What It Means to Be in an Interracial Relationship

Nick Yetto

Nick Yetto was a college student and a correspondent for Student.com, an Internet forum for teenagers, when he wrote the following article, wherein he describes how he came to realize he was involved in an interracial relationship only after noticing how others reacted to him and his Japanese girlfriend in public. Before this realization, he had not paid attention to the issue of race, thinking of his girlfriend more as someone from a different city than a different racial background.

Yetto believes he sees things more clearly now. He describes other relationships he's had since writing the original article and puts forth that culture, not race, has had the greatest impact on those relationships.

Seven years ago I wrote an article. It was titled "Race Relationships," and it was a brief waxing on my relationship with Tomoko (a pseudonym I'll use now, since she didn't appreciate her real name being used in the original). It was about a white college kid, *me*, dating a Japanese exchange student, and the small ways that race impacted us. Race wasn't our relationship's defining element—I'd like to think that love was, at least, good humor—but it was always there, lurking slightly off-screen, ready to make a strange entrance.

It wasn't a bad article. It was as good as I could do at the time, more personal essay than in-depth investigation, and it was honest. But it was an article about race—a whopper of a topic. My twelve-hundred words were more like a fart than an analysis; there are so many books on the subject that colleges offer programs dedicated to their study. I was admittedly out of my depth, and there I remain.

Tomoko, as I have said, is Asian. While we were dating, she was also a foreign exchange student, a stranger in a strange land, and also a dancer, a communications major, and a rabid Beatles fan. These where the things that we talked about. We dated for two-and-a-half years. I loved her deeply. We had great days and bad ones, fought stupidly and seriously, and it ended as most college romances do, at a semester's end. In the beginning, the racial differences where a surface-level intrigue. Tomoko is beautiful, and I found her beauty an exotic thing. Her accent was captivating, her use of English colorfully unpredictable. I was smitten. In our small, predominately white college, she was unique.

How much of my initial attraction can I lend to Tomoko's race? Quite a bit; it was part of what made her an interesting, attractive woman. But our relationship didn't feel like a profound experiment in racial mixing; we liked each other, we were attracted to one another, and we explored our feelings. Boy meets girl. Basic stuff.

Labeling a relationship as "interracial" or "biracial" is oversimplistic. If labels are necessary, a more apt term would be "intercultural," because that's really what's at the heart of the matter. In a black/white relationship, it's not a conflict of skin tone that causes people to stop and stare. It's the conspicuous conflict of cultures; the idea that a person with one set of values and loyalties would intimately connect with someone from a different, even conflicting, culture. To some, such a relationship represents a rejection of culture, as if by dating someone with a different heritage, you are turning your back on your own. Or worse—that you *prefer* the values of another culture. This is tribalism—an ugly relic of our primitive past. This remains an article about a white college kid dating a Japanese exchange student, so I'll steer clear of the cultural anthropology, but what I will say is this: Tribal thinking is much like the appendix; a primitive relic from our animal past; a protective mechanism for which there is no longer a need. Unlike the appendix, no surgery is required to remove racist thinking.

I have been in other serious relationships since. A few years back I dated a Chinese-American woman raised in suburban Michigan. More recently, I dated a Ukrainian woman studying in the United States. In the former, I was dating within my culture. She may have been Asian, but she was also from an affluent American family, from a small town much like the one I grew up in. Race felt like a total non-factor, and I can't recall it ever coming up. My relationship with the Ukrainian woman was far more like my relationship with Tomoko. To the outside world we were a typical white couple, but our personal lives where filled with cultural conflicts. We shared great moments of discovery, but our worldviews, which are so informed by the cultures in which we were raised, conflicted often. We are all products of our upbringing and experience, and this is the heaviest baggage that we carry into new relationships.

[This article] "Race Relationships" has taken on a life of its own. It was originally posted on a student magazine website, and since then I have received countless emails about it from people all over the world. The article has been reposted on other message boards and websites, and the chain of correspondence has continued. I'm still shocked by all of it. People have shared their own experiences with me, and I've been thanked many times for looking at the issue from a different angle. I have also been accused of being a partisan in a white conspiracy to steal Asian women away from Asian men. As I've said, race is a whopper of a topic.

What follows is the article, as it appeared in 1998. Only the aforementioned name has been changed. It is what it is—a snapshot of a relationship, a story about a boy and a girl. And when I think back with a bit of sad nostalgia, race doesn't figure in.

I'm the kind of guy that likes to play football video games and yell at the electronic referees. I chew with my mouth open. I sometimes pretend like I'm listening to someone when I'm really concentrating on a television program. I don't want to make myself out to be a slob, but I am a *guy*. Maybe that makes me a bit insensitive.

I've been with the same girl for over a year now. I've learned not to leave the toilet seat up, to avoid "things about you that bother me" conversations, and normally brush my teeth right after meals. It's basic stuff, as anyone in a long-term relationship will tell you. But overall I remain unchanged, and this whole relationship thing has been much less painful than I expected.

We're basically like every other couple in the United States, except for the fact that my girlfriend, Tomoko, is Japanese. She's studying in the U.S. and remains a citizen of her country. She speaks near-perfect English, fluent Japanese, and possesses the ability to move easily between both cultures. While she's different from other girls I've dated, it has never occurred to me that we were involved in an interracial relationship. Whenever I heard that term used, it had always referred to black and white couples. While I knew that Tomoko was Japanese, I never thought about it. Her being Asian was, in my mind, no different than being from another city.

But it meant something to her. As a minority in a predominately white school, issues of race have always been a consideration to her. "I want people to see me," she has said, "and not pre-judge me by the fact that I'm Japanese." She is the first to remind people that she's terrible at math, dislikes computers, and is not big fan of karaoke. Rather than just hanging out with other Janpese students, Tomoko has become close friends with American students. "That's how you learn about a culture" she insists. I laugh. I can't imagine American students having any culture at all.

Learning About Others' Experiences

I've discussed the issue with friends. I hoped that their experiences in biracial relationships could help me become a better boyfriend. Amy, a 22-year-old student from Los Angeles, was involved in an interracial relationship for over a year. She considers her time with Jesus, a native Colombian studying in the United States, her most serious relationship to date. She confesses that Latino men have always held a special attraction for her. "They tend to be very passionate about the women they love, about music and dance." She's attracted to men who can shake it on the dance floor, and likes the dark skin, hair, and eyes. Amy found the difference in culture more refreshing than discouraging but admits that there were times when it caused problems. "There were language barriers, not between Jesus and I, but with my friends and family. I was sometimes not included in conversations because I didn't speak Spanish. I kind of felt left out." All in all, she found the experience very satisfying. "It is amazing how much I learned about another culture and the experiences you go through while together."

Another friend, who asked to remain anonymous, had a different opinion. We'll call him Ray. Ray, a 20-year-old African-American student who attends State University of New York at Albany, has dated women from other races, but generally prefers that his girlfriends be black. "It's not worth the trouble" he told me. "I've been out with some great white girls, but there's always that thing." I asked him that he meant, although I had a pretty good idea. "You know, it's like there's something between you. As much as you might like each other, the race thing will always be there. It's not about skin color. It's a whole outlook on life." When I asked him if he's ever received disapproving looks or remarks, he laughed again. "Depending on where you are, you get that just for being black. If you have a white girl on your arm it's like, 'what is this guy doing to this innocent girl?' Sometimes you feel like a kidnapper."

I understood what Ray was saying, but I didn't feel it had any relevance for me. I knew that if I were dating a black girl, I would have realized from the beginning that I was in a biracial relationship. And everyone would agree. Tomoko is Japanese, however, and her being Asian seems less of definition of race than of culture. When I suggest to someone that we are a biracial couple, I'm more likely to receive a response like "well . . . I guess so."

Noticing Others' Reactions

It was at America's favorite restaurant that the truth became a little clearer to me. We were getting breakfast at McDonald's. When walking to our table we were regarded by a group of truck driver types who were languidly sipping coffee in the corner booth. All four of them stopped their conversation in mid-stream and looked at us. Stared, really. I didn't think anything of it—only that they were curious to see who was entering their hangout. I nodded to them and we found a booth.

"Did you see the way they looked at us?" Tomoko asked me, eyes wide.

"No." As I said, I didn't think anything of it. And I really didn't. I mean, people like to look at other people.

"They're probably wondering what a white boy is doing with an Asian" she said as she bit into her hash-browns.

"Maybe they're wondering what a hot chick like you is doing with a dork like me," I replied with sarcasm.

As our breakfast went on, I began to look at the situation differently. These men were shooting us sidelong glances, talking under their breath. It wasn't a profound, dramatic moment, but it was enough.

Seeing What I Had Been Missing

Now I see this all the time. Not so much when we're walking through campus, but when we're out in the world, holding hands, acting like sweethearts. Me, a 6'4", 230-pound white-boy, she a graceful 5'3" Asian. Our coupling might draw attention despite the different ethnicity, but sometimes the natural glances that we receive are too prolonged, the whispering comments too obvious. I don't know what these people are saying. Part of me would like to know, the other part would rather leave it alone.

I'm not surprised by this. I understand that racism still abounds, and despite our best efforts, there is little that can change the way people think. I cling to the hope that these stares and snickers are due to the fact that couples like Tomoko and I are uncommon. Many people, especially in small towns, see few interracial relationships. I hope their stares are out of curiosity and not disapproval. I don't care what they think, but it has opened my eyes. Ignorance is bliss, but it's also dangerous.

enses

hen almost a year went by. We started shar-
d other essays. Suddenly I wasn't just dealing
, I was dealing with a man. How could this
who practically caused a riot in a mall be-
walked into a store with a white girl? My
ily were shocked, and so was I. What was hap-
What was happening to us? What was I think-
o typical "white-boy". Not to say that he wasn't
that pseudo-vanilla-ice action [Vanilla Ice was
tist in the early 1990s] Scott was (and still is)
an All-American white guy—tall, blond hair,

st time in my life I was truly scared. I was afraid
I was feeling, afraid of everything I had believed
people, about black people, about interracial rela-
d issues of race. What was I willing to do, for the
ideologies about race? That is what my ideas had
eologies. Because now, here was a real person that
ne friends with, close friends with, and all my pre-
notions were crumbling each time we talked.

Loving a White Man

e I had three other roommates (we were in college,
I say?) There was a running pool on what would
ext. I was a mess. Did he like me, really? He had
ed to touch me, hold my hand or kiss me. Never
e a kiss or lingering hug. What would I do if he did
date? Would I say no? What about his parents? What
ine!
couldn't like me; I'd reassured my roommates and at-
d to reassure myself. I told them about a conversation
one day while shooting basketball together. In our
ary fashion he brought up a controversial subject. "You
a lot of pro-basketball players are married to white

Overcoming Racism Through Love

Tracey Sanford Crim

Tracey Sanford Crim, an African American woman who was raised in east Texas, currently resides in California with her Caucasian husband, Scott, and their infant son. She holds BAs in English and ethnic studies and an MA in women's studies. She is also a writer, an activist for racial and women's issues, and was recently on the Oprah Winfrey Show *with a panel of couples involved in interracial relationships.*

As a youth Crim experienced numerous racist incidents that hurt her deeply and caused her to be resentful and distrustful of other people, particularly whites. In the narrative that follows she describes how these wounds were healed as her friendship with Scott, a white classmate at her university, gradually deepened into love. This relationship helped her to dissolve her deep racial distrust and to enter into the loving marriage with him that she now enjoys.

I will never forget the day I realized what it meant to be black. My mother was a single parent of two young children. She joined the army with hopes that she would be able to scratch out a better life for us in the service. At the end of her tour, my sister and I returned with her to the small town in East Texas where she had been raised. To say that it was a difficult adjustment for me would be an understatement.

When we moved, I soon learned children stuck to their own kind. The black children and white children remained separated. I knew there were differences, knew that some people would probably not like me because of my race, but I had never been exposed to racism.

Tracey Sanford Crim, "Interracial Love Story," www.about.com, March 2003. Reproduced by permission of the author.

But with my "Northern" accent, as the white children said; my "proper" accent, as the black kids called it, I did not fit into any group. The loneliness and isolation would have been severe if one girl had not befriended me. She too was an outsider. She wore shabby clothes and large glasses that seemed to perpetually slide to the tip of her nose. Sometimes, she wore the same clothes more than one time in a week. Kids teased her and called her names, but none of this bothered me. So, I took up for her and she talked to me. I was glad to have a friend; I thought she was too.

Learning Racial Hatred

My mother had stopped at the local drug store on our way home. I was surprised and delighted when I saw my friend from school walking down an aisle toward me. I smiled immediately and called her name with a hello. But my greeting seemed to fall on deaf ears. I called her again as they got closer to me, still no answer. To this day, I don't remember how many times I called her name. Yet, the scene is as vivid in my mind as it was on that day. I can see her mother pulling her aside as they pass me standing in the middle of the aisle; I stood in shock and disbelief. Under her breath I heard her mother say as they brushed past me, "You know better than to be talking to them, we don't speak to those kind of people. . . ."

At eight years old I promised myself I would never care about another white person. I cried myself to sleep that night. My mother tried to comfort me as much as possible, told me people who were racist were ignorant. Later, out of anger, she told me, "We don't speak to those kind, either!" But nothing she could say could change the way I felt. My eyes were open— tainted. I experienced many other racist incidents and discrimination growing up there. Most were more severe. But this small event was a pivotal moment because it shaped how I saw people, specifically how I saw white people. I did not

and felt I coul
type of recipr
more.

Now Enter Sco

When Scott and I
English and Ethnic
University to have ;
out calling it that. \
At our next meeting,
me. It took three mo
name.

I was very interestec
a mutual love for debate
sharing our views and c
have always been a passi
match. Our "discussions" c
played devil's advocate, si
sake of the debate. A more
this annoying, but I enjoyed

Over time, we found ours
not only on the issues of race
cies were challenged at my Uni
opposing and supporting viev
stump him when it came to rac
about W.E.B. DuBois [African A
who founded the National Assoc
of Colored People]? What could
Garvey [proponent of Black Natior
Universal Negro Improvement Assoc
colm X's autobiography in 10th grac
cetera, et cetera, et cetera. . . . Each tir
become an issue, it was not an issue,
issue.

Crumbling Def

Months passed, t
ing our poetry ar
with a white ma
be, from the gir
cause a brother
friends and fam
pening to me?
ing? Scott was
white, none of
a white rap ar
the picture o
and blue-eyed

For the fi
of everything
about white
tionships an
sake of my
become—id
I had becoi
conceived

Afraid o

At the tir
what can
happen
never tr
given m
want to
about 1

He
tempte
we ha
custor
know

women." (It was understood he was referring to black basketball players marrying white women.) He asked me what I thought about interracial dating. I knew he had dated interracially before. He had dated almost every ethnicity available, white, black, Hispanic, Asian. . . . I responded quickly, not thinking of him, "It's not for me." That had been months ago and the subject never resurfaced. Surely, he got the Message . . . but did I really want him to get the message? What if he thought of me as some experiment, you know, sow your wild oats kind of thing? But nothing he had ever done or said had given me that impression. I knew him that well.

I decided that I would not call him. Which didn't matter—he called me. I needed some time to get myself together, needed to stop tripping, as my girlfriends said. I told him I was busy for a couple of days. I was miserable wondering where he was, what he was doing; we were still "just friends." It was true—I had it bad for a man who had never tried to hold my hand!

Scott's Confession of Love

One of my roommates answered the phone when he called. I took my time coming to the phone, trying my best to put on my "buddy" voice. He played along with me as if the fact we had not seen each other in a week was commonplace. I felt sick. My heart was beating erratically, my palms were sweating, and my mouth was dry. . . . All I wanted was for us to go back to the way we were, before I discovered I was in love with my best friend, the white guy. We talked about nothing, and I felt I was going to make it and end the conversation without making a complete fool of myself by blurting out something stupid like, "I love you."

But instead he changed the conversation.

"We've been knowing each other for a while, now, right?"

"Yeah," I breathed. Where's he going with this?

"We know each other well, right?"

"Yeah, I guess." Oh, my God! Panic was rising into my throat, now. My eyes raced around the apartment. Frantically, I waved my arms to attract my roommates' attention. Terra was lying on the floor in front of the TV. Debbie was almost comatose on the sofa. Tamera was in the dining room with one eye on a textbook and another on the TV. They watched my jerking movements in awe. I motioned, "Shhhh."

"You know my favorite color, right? What's my favorite color?"

"You don't have a favorite color."

"Just checking. And I know yours, hot pink."

"Okay."

"We know each other well."

"Okay . . ." I couldn't breathe.

"You trust me, Tracey?"

"Yes." Why did he say my name that way? He'd never said it that way before.

"We know each other well, but I'd like us to get to know each other. I want to know you. I'm not talking about just as friends."

"Oh, okay." My mouth dropped.

"I don't want an answer now. I just want you to think about it. You don't have to be afraid, Tracey. I'm not going to hurt you. You're the kind of woman that I've wanted all my life and all I want is a chance, a chance to show you, to make you see I'm real. . . . No games, just me and you."

Transformed by Love

I couldn't speak. I could feel tears in my eyes. He knew about everything now. I couldn't pretend, couldn't shrug off his assessments; he knew me too well. We had talked about almost everything in our lives. Our parents, our broken homes, our failed relationships . . . we had no secrets; he was my best friend.

"But what about our families, your family, my family?" I whispered.

"We'll deal with that when it comes, but now this is between us."

"Okay. Okay, Scott, but we have to take it slow ... I—I've never—"

"I know, baby, neither have I." He didn't have to finish the sentence.

How could I refuse? How could I reject the person who knew me so well, who was so close to my heart—just because he was the wrong color? That night the hate that had hardened my heart, kept me closed and angry, melted away. His love for me changed me. I have come to realize the only weapon against hatred is love and the only weapon against anger is kindness. Hate can only be destroyed by a love that goes beyond us, beyond self.

Choosing to Love Beyond the Scars of History

Four years later we were married in a beautiful church ceremony. All of our parents and stepparents were there and Scott's family outnumbered mine. He had told me they would love and accept me. And though I still find it hard to believe sometimes, he was right; it seems they have. That was almost three years ago.

Sometimes, I stop to think about the odds that are against us and the odds that we would find each other, end up together. I think about if we had been born in a different time than now. In those times, our love seems even more precious, because we never take one another for granted. We are only together because we chose one another. We still live one day at a time, handling the prejudice we face as it comes—but honestly, Scott taking out the trash and me balancing the checkbook are usually greater issues. When it is all said and done, we are just an average couple, a man and a woman who chose to love beyond the constraints of culture and the scars of history.

Sharing Cultural Differences Enriches Interracial Love

Jennifer Guintu

Jennifer Guintu is a young Filipina woman from Newbury Park, California. At the time she wrote the following essay she was a first-year student at the University of Notre Dame.

Looking back on her adolescence growing up in a predominantly white culture, Guintu recalls being confused and conflicted about her identity. On the one hand, she was attracted to Caucasian boys but felt unattractive because of her Asian appearance and culture. On the other hand, she worried about being rejected by other Filipinos for not being Filipino enough.

Guintu describes how her interracial dating experiences have helped her to become more confident about her own identity while also learning about other people's cultures. In her opinion cultural or racial backgrounds should not stand in the way of relationships. When interracial couples are willing to share their traditions with each other rather than trying to suppress their differences, interracial love can be colorful as well as color-blind.

"He's got a nice booty, a six pack, blond hair, blue-eyes. Oh! And he's tan from surfing." That is the ideal boy among the girls with whom I have grown up.

Yet my relatives tell me, "Don't marry an American (meaning Caucasian) because you'll only end up in divorce."

But there are very few Filipinos and minorities in Newbury Park, California. And when I gather with other Filipinos, I am considered "white washed" because of where I live and the way I dress and talk.

However, when I am around Caucasian boys, I feel unattractive because I look different. So basically, I am stuck.

Jennifer Guintu, "Make the Decision to Be Colorblind," Notre Dame University's *Observer Online*, March 1, 2000. Reproduced by permission.

Those are the feelings of the confused adolescent I used to be. At times I would wonder if I was not trying hard enough to suppress my Filipino heritage in order to seem more normal and, therefore, more attractive. At other times I would wonder if I was Filipino enough to be accepted by my "own kind."

Race Does Not Make the Person

Dating men of other races has helped me to clear up my confusion on interracial dating. I had always considered interracial dating a good thing because it seemed natural to me—my mother is half-Italian, half-Filipino and my siblings and cousins prefer to date Caucasians.

But only recently through my experiences have I developed a more in-depth opinion on this issue: While heritage adds to a person and his or her character, it does not make the person.

Race or ethnicity can add to a relationship, but it does not make the relationship. Rather, personality and character is what should draw two people together. Racial differences should not limit a person from discovering a beautiful and compatible companion.

Family Attitudes

While my family has tended to have a bias towards same-race dating, it has been accepting of interracial dating with Caucasians.

My aunt has been married to an Irish man for more than 20 years. Looking at their relationship, I find it encouraging because my aunt does not suppress her Filipino upbringing to be more compatible with her husband.

Rather, my uncle embraces the Filipino culture and attempts to learn as much as he can about his wife's heritage. My uncle, out of love, has stepped outside his "comfort zone" and in return my family has accepted him.

Family Pressure

However, family can often add tension to an interracial relationship. I remember my relatives' reaction to my first boyfriend, who was Persian.

"Be careful, they don't treat women right."

"He might seem nice now, but just be careful."

Much of this ignorance came from the media, but it was difficult bringing him into the family. I became a threat to his family, too. His father would threaten to stop paying his college tuition if he continued to see me.

Apparently his father felt that "Filipinos are disgraceful Christians who mistreat Muslims."

I had never felt so enraged and so misunderstood. Rather than letting the anger get the better of me, though, I used it in a positive manner.

Sharing and Respecting Heritage

During that relationship, and during subsequent relationships, I shared Filipino customs, traditions and foods with those I dated. In the process, I learned more about who I am and became prouder of my heritage.

In return, it has been just as important to learn about my partners' heritage. Personally, I have always had an affinity towards cultural awareness and learning about new people and traditions.

Learning about a partner's heritage helps me to understand him better as a person. Moreover, my family and friends learn to be more understanding and accepting.

By advocating interracial relationships, I am also advocating cultural awareness. Yet as I stated earlier, heritage does not make a person; it adds to his or her character.

Geographic upbringing and the demographics of your environment also are strong influences on one's personality and interests. My sister considers herself more compatible with a Caucasian (blond hair, blue-eyed) man from the suburbs than she does with a Filipino who grew up in the city. When looking at my sister's relationship, I have observed that she is with her boyfriend not because of his race but because of their common interests—interests that have been influenced by their geographic upbringing.

Colorblind or Colorful?

"Love is colorblind."

I'm sure you've heard that before, but have you really thought about that statement? Sometimes I think we create boundaries and set limits on love. While love itself is colorblind, the love between two people can be colorful.

Sharing cultural differences and embracing diversity makes relationships richer. It can also add to the excitement of dating. However, it is easy to assume things about people based on their appearances.

Setting mental boundaries prevents me (or anyone) from a wonderful and even life-changing encounter. I find it more fulfilling getting to know people rather than avoiding race.

Overcoming Racism Through Love

Tracey Sanford Crim

Tracey Sanford Crim, an African American woman who was raised in east Texas, currently resides in California with her Caucasian husband, Scott, and their infant son. She holds BAs in English and ethnic studies and an MA in women's studies. She is also a writer, an activist for racial and women's issues, and was recently on the Oprah Winfrey Show *with a panel of couples involved in interracial relationships.*

As a youth Crim experienced numerous racist incidents that hurt her deeply and caused her to be resentful and distrustful of other people, particularly whites. In the narrative that follows she describes how these wounds were healed as her friendship with Scott, a white classmate at her university, gradually deepened into love. This relationship helped her to dissolve her deep racial distrust and to enter into the loving marriage with him that she now enjoys.

I will never forget the day I realized what it meant to be black. My mother was a single parent of two young children. She joined the army with hopes that she would be able to scratch out a better life for us in the service. At the end of her tour, my sister and I returned with her to the small town in East Texas where she had been raised. To say that it was a difficult adjustment for me would be an understatement.

When we moved, I soon learned children stuck to their own kind. The black children and white children remained separated. I knew there were differences, knew that some people would probably not like me because of my race, but I had never been exposed to racism.

Tracey Sanford Crim, "Interracial Love Story," www.about.com, March 2003. Reproduced by permission of the author.

But with my "Northern" accent, as the white children said; my "proper" accent, as the black kids called it, I did not fit into any group. The loneliness and isolation would have been severe if one girl had not befriended me. She too was an outsider. She wore shabby clothes and large glasses that seemed to perpetually slide to the tip of her nose. Sometimes, she wore the same clothes more than one time in a week. Kids teased her and called her names, but none of this bothered me. So, I took up for her and she talked to me. I was glad to have a friend; I thought she was too.

Learning Racial Hatred

My mother had stopped at the local drug store on our way home. I was surprised and delighted when I saw my friend from school walking down an aisle toward me. I smiled immediately and called her name with a hello. But my greeting seemed to fall on deaf ears. I called her again as they got closer to me, still no answer. To this day, I don't remember how many times I called her name. Yet, the scene is as vivid in my mind as it was on that day. I can see her mother pulling her aside as they pass me standing in the middle of the aisle; I stood in shock and disbelief. Under her breath I heard her mother say as they brushed past me, "You know better than to be talking to them, we don't speak to those kind of people. . . ."

At eight years old I promised myself I would never care about another white person. I cried myself to sleep that night. My mother tried to comfort me as much as possible, told me people who were racist were ignorant. Later, out of anger, she told me, "We don't speak to those kind, either!" But nothing she could say could change the way I felt. My eyes were open—tainted. I experienced many other racist incidents and discrimination growing up there. Most were more severe. But this small event was a pivotal moment because it shaped how I saw people, specifically how I saw white people. I did not and felt I could not trust white people. I resigned myself to a type of reciprocal hatred. If they hated me, I'd hate them more.

Now Enter Scott

When Scott and I met, I was a junior in college majoring in English and Ethnic Studies. Ethnic Studies was a way for the University to have an African-American Studies degree without calling it that. We actually met through a mutual friend. At our next meeting, to my chagrin, Scott did not remember me. It took three meetings before he could remember my name.

I was very interested in social politics and Scott and I had a mutual love for debate. Our friendship began with us simply sharing our views and opinions about the world and life. I have always been a passionate person; in Scott I found my match. Our "discussions" often lasted until sunrise. Scott often played devil's advocate, siding with controversy just for the sake of the debate. A more timid person might have found this annoying, but I enjoyed every moment!

Over time, we found ourselves agreeing on the issues, and not only on the issues of race. When affirmative action policies were challenged at my University, he understood both the opposing and supporting views. I found myself trying to stump him when it came to race issues. What do you know about W.E.B. DuBois [African American scholar and activist who founded the National Association for the Advancement of Colored People]? What could you know about Marcus Garvey [proponent of Black Nationalism and founder of the Universal Negro Improvement Association]? So you read Malcolm X's autobiography in 10th grade . . . What about . . . et cetera, et cetera, et cetera. . . . Each time race could potentially become an issue, it was not an issue, until it became a "non" issue.

Crumbling Defenses

Months passed, then almost a year went by. We started sharing our poetry and other essays. Suddenly I wasn't just dealing with a white man, I was dealing with a man. How could this be, from the girl who practically caused a riot in a mall because a brother walked into a store with a white girl? My friends and family were shocked, and so was I. What was happening to me? What was happening to us? What was I thinking? Scott was no typical "white-boy". Not to say that he wasn't white, none of that pseudo-vanilla-ice action [Vanilla Ice was a white rap artist in the early 1990s] Scott was (and still is) the picture of an All-American white guy—tall, blond hair, and blue-eyed.

For the first time in my life I was truly scared. I was afraid of everything I was feeling, afraid of everything I had believed about white people, about black people, about interracial relationships and issues of race. What was I willing to do, for the sake of my ideologies about race? That is what my ideas had become—ideologies. Because now, here was a real person that I had become friends with, close friends with, and all my preconceived notions were crumbling each time we talked.

Afraid of Loving a White Man

At the time I had three other roommates (we were in college, what can I say?) There was a running pool on what would happen next. I was a mess. Did he like me, really? He had never tried to touch me, hold my hand or kiss me. Never given me a kiss or lingering hug. What would I do if he did want to date? Would I say no? What about his parents? What about mine!

He couldn't like me; I'd reassured my roommates and attempted to reassure myself. I told them about a conversation we had one day while shooting basketball together. In our customary fashion he brought up a controversial subject. "You know, a lot of pro-basketball players are married to white women." (It was understood he was referring to black basketball players marrying white women.) He asked me what I thought about interracial dating. I knew he had dated interracially before. He had dated almost every ethnicity available, white, black, Hispanic, Asian. . . . I responded quickly, not thinking of him, "It's not for me." That had been months ago and the subject never resurfaced. Surely, he got the Message . . . but did I really want him to get the message? What if he thought of me as some experiment, you know, sow your wild oats kind of thing? But nothing he had ever done or said had given me that impression. I knew him that well.

I decided that I would not call him. Which didn't matter—he called me. I needed some time to get myself together, needed to stop tripping, as my girlfriends said. I told him I was busy for a couple of days. I was miserable wondering where he was, what he was doing; we were still "just friends." It was true—I had it bad for a man who had never tried to hold my hand!

Scott's Confession of Love

One of my roommates answered the phone when he called. I took my time coming to the phone, trying my best to put on my "buddy" voice. He played along with me as if the fact we had not seen each other in a week was commonplace. I felt sick. My heart was beating erratically, my palms were sweating, and my mouth was dry. . . . All I wanted was for us to go back to the way we were, before I discovered I was in love with my best friend, the white guy. We talked about nothing, and I felt I was going to make it and end the conversation without making a complete fool of myself by blurting out something stupid like, "I love you."

But instead he changed the conversation.

"We've been knowing each other for a while, now, right?"

"Yeah," I breathed. Where's he going with this?

"We know each other well, right?"

"Yeah, I guess." Oh, my God! Panic was rising into my throat, now. My eyes raced around the apartment. Frantically, I waved my arms to attract my roommates' attention. Terra was lying on the floor in front of the TV. Debbie was almost comatose on the sofa. Tamera was in the dining room with one eye on a textbook and another on the TV. They watched my jerking movements in awe. I motioned, "Shhhh."

"You know my favorite color, right? What's my favorite color?"

"You don't have a favorite color."

"Just checking. And I know yours, hot pink."

"Okay."

"We know each other well."

"Okay . . ." I couldn't breathe.

"You trust me, Tracey?"

"Yes." Why did he say my name that way? He'd never said it that way before.

"We know each other well, but I'd like us to get to know each other. I want to know you. I'm not talking about just as friends."

"Oh, okay." My mouth dropped.

"I don't want an answer now. I just want you to think about it. You don't have to be afraid, Tracey. I'm not going to hurt you. You're the kind of woman that I've wanted all my life and all I want is a chance, a chance to show you, to make you see I'm real. . . . No games, just me and you."

Transformed by Love

I couldn't speak. I could feel tears in my eyes. He knew about everything now. I couldn't pretend, couldn't shrug off his assessments; he knew me too well. We had talked about almost everything in our lives. Our parents, our broken homes, our failed relationships . . . we had no secrets; he was my best friend.

"But what about our families, your family, my family?" I whispered.

"We'll deal with that when it comes, but now this is between us."

"Okay. Okay, Scott, but we have to take it slow . . . I—I've never—"

"I know, baby, neither have I." He didn't have to finish the sentence.

How could I refuse? How could I reject the person who knew me so well, who was so close to my heart—just because he was the wrong color? That night the hate that had hardened my heart, kept me closed and angry, melted away. His love for me changed me. I have come to realize the only weapon against hatred is love and the only weapon against anger is kindness. Hate can only be destroyed by a love that goes beyond us, beyond self.

Choosing to Love Beyond the Scars of History

Four years later we were married in a beautiful church ceremony. All of our parents and stepparents were there and Scott's family outnumbered mine. He had told me they would love and accept me. And though I still find it hard to believe sometimes, he was right; it seems they have. That was almost three years ago.

Sometimes, I stop to think about the odds that are against us and the odds that we would find each other, end up together. I think about if we had been born in a different time than now. In those times, our love seems even more precious, because we never take one another for granted. We are only together because we chose one another. We still live one day at a time, handling the prejudice we face as it comes—but honestly, Scott taking out the trash and me balancing the checkbook are usually greater issues. When it is all said and done, we are just an average couple, a man and a woman who chose to love beyond the constraints of culture and the scars of history.

Sharing Cultural Differences Enriches Interracial Love

Jennifer Guintu

Jennifer Guintu is a young Filipina woman from Newbury Park, California. At the time she wrote the following essay she was a first-year student at the University of Notre Dame.

Looking back on her adolescence growing up in a predominantly white culture, Guintu recalls being confused and conflicted about her identity. On the one hand, she was attracted to Caucasian boys but felt unattractive because of her Asian appearance and culture. On the other hand, she worried about being rejected by other Filipinos for not being Filipino enough.

Guintu describes how her interracial dating experiences have helped her to become more confident about her own identity while also learning about other people's cultures. In her opinion cultural or racial backgrounds should not stand in the way of relationships. When interracial couples are willing to share their traditions with each other rather than trying to suppress their differences, interracial love can be colorful as well as color-blind.

"He's got a nice booty, a six pack, blond hair, blue-eyes. Oh! And he's tan from surfing." That is the ideal boy among the girls with whom I have grown up.

Yet my relatives tell me, "Don't marry an American (meaning Caucasian) because you'll only end up in divorce."

But there are very few Filipinos and minorities in Newbury Park, California. And when I gather with other Filipinos, I am considered "white washed" because of where I live and the way I dress and talk.

However, when I am around Caucasian boys, I feel unattractive because I look different. So basically, I am stuck.

Jennifer Guintu, "Make the Decision to Be Colorblind," Notre Dame University's *Observer Online*, March 1, 2000. Reproduced by permission.

Those are the feelings of the confused adolescent I used to be. At times I would wonder if I was not trying hard enough to suppress my Filipino heritage in order to seem more normal and, therefore, more attractive. At other times I would wonder if I was Filipino enough to be accepted by my "own kind."

Race Does Not Make the Person

Dating men of other races has helped me to clear up my confusion on interracial dating. I had always considered interracial dating a good thing because it seemed natural to me—my mother is half-Italian, half-Filipino and my siblings and cousins prefer to date Caucasians.

But only recently through my experiences have I developed a more in-depth opinion on this issue: While heritage adds to a person and his or her character, it does not make the person.

Race or ethnicity can add to a relationship, but it does not make the relationship. Rather, personality and character is what should draw two people together. Racial differences should not limit a person from discovering a beautiful and compatible companion.

Family Attitudes

While my family has tended to have a bias towards same-race dating, it has been accepting of interracial dating with Caucasians.

My aunt has been married to an Irish man for more than 20 years. Looking at their relationship, I find it encouraging because my aunt does not suppress her Filipino upbringing to be more compatible with her husband.

Rather, my uncle embraces the Filipino culture and attempts to learn as much as he can about his wife's heritage. My uncle, out of love, has stepped outside his "comfort zone" and in return my family has accepted him.

Family Pressure

However, family can often add tension to an interracial relationship. I remember my relatives' reaction to my first boyfriend, who was Persian.

"Be careful, they don't treat women right."

"He might seem nice now, but just be careful."

Much of this ignorance came from the media, but it was difficult bringing him into the family. I became a threat to his family, too. His father would threaten to stop paying his college tuition if he continued to see me.

Apparently his father felt that "Filipinos are disgraceful Christians who mistreat Muslims."

I had never felt so enraged and so misunderstood. Rather than letting the anger get the better of me, though, I used it in a positive manner.

Sharing and Respecting Heritage

During that relationship, and during subsequent relationships, I shared Filipino customs, traditions and foods with those I dated. In the process, I learned more about who I am and became prouder of my heritage.

In return, it has been just as important to learn about my partners' heritage. Personally, I have always had an affinity towards cultural awareness and learning about new people and traditions.

Learning about a partner's heritage helps me to understand him better as a person. Moreover, my family and friends learn to be more understanding and accepting.

By advocating interracial relationships, I am also advocating cultural awareness. Yet as I stated earlier, heritage does not make a person; it adds to his or her character.

Geographic upbringing and the demographics of your environment also are strong influences on one's personality and interests. My sister considers herself more compatible with a Caucasian (blond hair, blue-eyed) man from the suburbs than she does with a Filipino who grew up in the city. When looking at my sister's relationship, I have observed that she is with her boyfriend not because of his race but because of their common interests—interests that have been influenced by their geographic upbringing.

Colorblind or Colorful?

"Love is colorblind."

I'm sure you've heard that before, but have you really thought about that statement? Sometimes I think we create boundaries and set limits on love. While love itself is colorblind, the love between two people can be colorful.

Sharing cultural differences and embracing diversity makes relationships richer. It can also add to the excitement of dating. However, it is easy to assume things about people based on their appearances.

Setting mental boundaries prevents me (or anyone) from a wonderful and even life-changing encounter. I find it more fulfilling getting to know people rather than avoiding race.

Questioning Interracial Dating Trends Among Asian Americans

Helen E. Sung

Noting that Asian American women tend to marry interracially more often than women from other racial backgrounds, writer Helen E. Sung reflected on her own dating habits and was embarrassed to find how few Asian men she had dated. This realization inspired her to interview her Asian friends and acquaintances about their dating habits. She was surprised to learn that many of them, both women and men, had never seriously dated another Asian.

In the essay that follows, Sung explores this trend and reflects on the reasons behind it. She agrees with one of her friends that race should not be an issue in matters of love, but she is curious about the sense of embarrassment she feels for not having dated more Asians. Among those she spoke with, many reasons were given for their interracial dating habits—that they were not attracted to other Asians, or that Asian women were too Americanized and independent, or that Asian men expected women to be too traditional and subservient. Desiring to understand this issue better, Sung also sought out the advice of several Asian sociologists, some of whom considered the trend to be a natural result of demographics, with Asians still composing a small percentage of the U.S. population. Others suggested that Asian Americans have unknowingly taken on the racist attitudes of the predominant white culture or allowed themselves to be fetishized and exoticized by whites.

"What do you mean by 'dated?'" asks my friend Claire [all names of interviewees have been changed], a Korean American graduate student who is living with her boyfriend, who is white, when I ask her one night over drinks if she has ever dated an Asian guy.

"You know, something more than a couple of dates," I explain. "It doesn't have to have been a boyfriend, but someone you at least went out with for a while."

Claire pauses and takes a thoughtful sip of her gin and tonic while I look at her expectantly.

"Well, there was this one guy," she begins, launching into a story about a Korean American guy she had known at one time, who was good-looking, they were friends and hung out all the time.

"So did you ever go out with him?" I cut in.

"No."

"Why not?"

"I don't know. It would've been weird," she says, looking uncomfortable. When I press her for details, she squirms, looks away, takes another sip of her drink, sighs and finally takes a stab at an explanation.

A Question of Expectations

"I grew up in a really WASP-y [white Anglo-Saxon Protestant] environment," she explains. "My parents [who are Korean] sent me to boarding school in Connecticut, where everybody was white. I thought if I dated a Korean guy, I would have to marry him, that I just couldn't mess around and have fun."

"But with white guys, you felt like you could just hook up and have a good time and not let it be anything serious?" I asked. "Exactly," she said, looking relieved that I seemed to understand.

But I didn't really understand. There seemed to be something deeper going on, something to do with her having grown up in an all white environment, but I didn't want to push it.

We were getting into issues of race, sexuality, self-image, attraction, and it was touchy territory.

A Perplexing Pattern

By now, I don't need to state the obvious: we Asian women marry outside our race at far greater rates than any other racial group, the most frequent being the Asian female/white male combination. Maybe it was the potential of feeling like a mere statistic or walking cliché that prompted me a few years ago to take stock of my dating history. Bracing myself, I realized that I had pretty much dated the rainbow, with the glaring exception of Asian men (only a few dates over the years) and the notable over-representation of white men.

Admitting the above, I know, does not endear me to my Asian brothers. I still remember the expression on my Chinese American friend John's face when I told him a few years ago that I had begun dating someone. "Is he Asian?" asked John, looking at me hopefully. I had to answer truthfully "no" as I watched John's face fall.

Exactly how many other women are out there like me is unclear. None of the psychologists and sociologists I spoke with was aware of a study that measured the percentage of AA [Asian American] women, and men, who have never dated another Asian. "Let me know if you do come across any research on that," each of the experts told me. If there is such a study, it's probably buried in a graduate school thesis somewhere that has yet to see the light of day.

My own highly unscientific study—namely, empirical observations and talking to friends, acquaintances, colleagues and people at parties—indicates that I am not alone. Far from it. Besides my friend Claire, I know several other AA women who have never dated another Asian, and in the course of writing this article, I met more—including a surprising number of men. Almost everyone I talked to, Asian and non-Asian said, "Oh, I know someone like that." or "I know someone you should talk to" when I told them the subject of my article.

I'm Just Not Attracted to Asians

I hear lots of different reasons from AAs for why they haven't dated other Asians. "I'm just not attracted to Asian guys," says Reesa, a 32-year-old Filipino American who lives in Northern California. "I don't know why. I just never have been. I've just always dated white or European guys."

Tina, a 31-year-old Chinese American who grew up in an ethnically mixed community in Texas, dated Asians in high school, but stopped when she got to college. "The Asian guys are either too traditional and expect an Asian girl who is more obedient, subservient and domesticated. Or at the other extreme, they are too Americanized and have lost their cultural values and are superficial and materialistic."

She laments that it's hard to find an Asian guy who is "truly bicultural" like her, i.e., very Americanized, but still valuing her Chinese heritage. "Asian guys can't deal with a woman who is independent," she says. "They want a woman who will take care of them and cook and clean for them. I still see that in Asian couples, where the girl does the domestic chores."

A Growing Trend

Lately, Tina has been dating Jewish men, a growing trend, at least in New York City. "I know of a lot of Jewish guy/Asian girl couples," Tina says. "And it makes sense because our cultures share a lot of the same upbringing and family values."

"I've never been attracted to Asian women," says Tony, 33, a Japanese American who grew up in an all white environment near Philadelphia. "My type is a blonde-haired girl," he says. "Blondes have caught my eye for some reason."

Kelly, a Korean American in her mid-30s who grew up in Los Angeles, prefers dating non-Asian men because she feels less inhibited around them. "With Asian guys, I feel like I have to be super feminine and docile. I feel like I can't be as sexually free as I can with non-Asian guys."

"Asian guys don't ask me out," says Sara, a Korean American in her late 20s. "When I'm out [at night at a bar], I'll see Asian guys looking at me, but they won't come over. They'll just stare from across the room. I always get hit on by white guys."

Why Does It Matter?

On paper, Dave is every Asian mother's dream for their daughter: a physician, educated at the most elite institutions in the country, Korean American, handsome, fit and still single at 34. Except for one thing. Dave doesn't date Asian women. He has only dated white women. When I ask him about it, he's genuinely perplexed. "I don't get it," he says, about finding it "inherently suspicious" that someone has not dated within his or her own race. "It seems overly critical and not really necessary. There is all this hand wringing that two-culture people have about their identity. They question, 'Is there something wrong with me?' 'Are you a traitor to your race?' Because there would be no question if you only dated Asians."

True. Asians dating Asians does not draw the scrutiny, or even interest, that Asians exclusively dating whites does. It seems natural and expected that if you're Asian, you'll date another Asian. (I realize there are huge differences between the Asian ethnicities—including dating patterns and even stereotypes that we hold about each other—but that's a whole other article.)

"What does it matter what race the person is that you're with?" asks my best friend, Gina, an Italian American who subscribes to the "people are people" school of thought. "As long as you care about each other, that's all that should matter."

I couldn't agree with her more. People should feel free to date whomever they want. It's hard enough finding someone you're compatible with, so it seems silly to artificially narrow your dating choices to a racial group or ethnicity.

But it still strikes me as odd that Dave has never gone out with an Asian woman, despite having grown up in Los Angeles and professing to being "open to dating whomever." And what about AA women like Claire and me? Why did we feel a vague sense of embarrassment that we had never really dated an Asian man, as if it somehow communicated something, probably negative, about us? Maybe it doesn't mean anything, but surely the situations merit some analysis.

The Socioeconomics of Dating

"Why a relatively high proportion of many Asian Americans intermarry and with whom they intermarry are sociologically important and interesting questions," Sara S. Lee, Ph.D., assistant professor of sociology at Kent State University, writes to me in a recent email. "However, I do not think it is odd for an Asian American in the United States to have never dated another Asian or to marry a non-Asian (i.e., white) person."

Lee points to factors such as population size, socioeconomic status and proximity. Given that Asian Americans comprise a mere 4.3 percent of the total U.S. population, it's not surprising we would intermarry. Studies also show that the higher the level of education and occupation, the more likely for an AA to intermarry. "If Asian Americans live, attend schools and/or work mostly among white Americans, chances are, they will most likely marry white Americans," writes Lee.

Those are Dave's reasons for never having dated an Asian woman, despite having lived in Los Angeles and currently living in San Francisco—both cities with large populations of Asians. "Being Asian American and professional, we move among whites and we're able to navigate through those worlds. It's socioeconomic. We're always surrounded by whites.

"My friends have asked why I don't date Asian women and I joke that maybe they remind me too much of my mom," Dave continues. He grew up in an upper middle class predominantly white neighborhood in West Los Angeles. He attended an exclusive boys' school. He never socialized or hung out in Koreatown. In college, he got involved with the Korean Students Association, eventually becoming an officer, and had Asian friends. But he admits he was "not particularly attracted to Asian women." . . .

Manufactured Desire

"Your physical and sexual attraction is socially constructed," says Elaine Kim, Ph.D., professor of Asian American Studies at the University of California at Berkeley, "and it's hard to escape from that." If you're Asian, the way you see yourself and the way you think about beauty, according to Kim, is very different if you went to high school in Monterey Park (a community in Los Angeles County with a large Asian population), where the kids voted most popular, the most beautiful were Asian, versus going to a high school where everyone is blonde-haired and blue-eyed.

Karen, a 32-year-old Korean American who has dated mostly white men, readily admits she's been affected by her environment. Growing up in a predominantly white town in Southern California, the only Asian males in her life were either related to her (father, brothers, cousins) or were the men at church. "I didn't see Asian guys in a sexual way when I was growing up," she says. It didn't help that the only images she saw of Asian males in the media were of cringe-inducing geeks like Long Duck Dong in the teen flick, *Sixteen Candles*, or the strangely asexual and decidedly unattractive David Carradine character in the television series, *Kung Fu*.

"I just don't find Asian guys attractive," Karen says. "They're usually short and slight and don't seem confident."

The Impact of Stereotypes

Negative stereotypes and images of Asian males in the media have had a real impact on the dating choices of AAs, according to Lee. In a study she conducted among Korean Americans in New York, the men reported that they had little choice but to date Asian women because non-Asian women were not attracted to them. Many of the Korean American women in the study believed the negative images of AA men as nerdy and sexually undesirable. This was especially true if, like Karen, the women had little contact with Asians growing up and their views were largely shaped by movies and television shows.

"Television and other media act as 'cultural propaganda,' powerful social institutions shaping racialized views in both overt and covert ways," says Lee. "These 'controlling images' also influence some Asian Americans to have negative racial views of themselves." . . .

Racist Love

According to [Asian American Studies professor Darrell] Hamamoto, the process starts as soon as you're born. Asians already come from countries that have been dominated by white people, such as Hong Kong, Taiwan, South Korea and Japan, he says. Against this backdrop, "you're exposed to media garbage and Hollywood productions like the *Last Samurai* where the white guy, Tom Cruise, is the hero. That's ridiculous, but that's how you grow up. You're given signals that white people are better physically, intellectually, spiritually."

When it comes to Asian men who exclusively date white women, Hamamoto says "they are so desperate to be accepted [by whites] that being with a white woman is their entrée."

He is even more scathing when it comes to Asian women who only date white men, asserting that they are unaware of the history of what he calls "racist love." Asian women in America started to get fetishized, he asserts, as a result of relaxed immigration barriers in 1965 that created a large-scale influx of Asians to the States. At the same time, you had a generation of white American men who had been in Vietnam and experienced Asian prostitutes, and who now had a larger pool of AA women.

"When you have Asian American women [who are] ignorant of that history and that the desire from these people goes back to the colonization of Asian countries, the media portrayal of Asian women, and Asian American women being socialized into the white supremacist world of media, it makes perfect sense," Hamamoto says. "Underlying it all is a form of racist love, not an equality."

What he says next is even more startling. "These Asian American women get hit on or propositioned by white men, but they don't realize what lies beneath; that they're coming onto you as a prostitute or massage woman, because that's what they see, first and foremost, regardless of educational level. Conversely, an Asian American woman in white supremacist America will value anything white. I won't say it's instinctual, but almost at the preconscious level."

Whiteness Is the Norm

Kim's comments are similar. "Whiteness has a centrality; it is the highest point in the hierarchy," she explains. "Whiteness is taken as the norm against which everyone else is measured and you couldn't help but buy into it."

"Growing up around whites," she remembers, "I was shocked when I walked by a mirror and saw my Asian reflection." She felt brainwashed by a white society that told her people like her were ugly and inferior. "I had to purge myself of that thought," she says, explaining why she no longer dates white men, despite having been married to one. "If I went out with a white guy, I'd be going back to that. It's my problem," she acknowledges, "but I don't want to be in that situation again."

So, are the experts saying never to date white men?

No. Even Hamamoto won't say that. "I really don't care. People can live their lives however," he says. "But both Asian American men and women need to be made aware of where desire comes from, how desire is produced and how we human beings internalize it."

Interracial Couples Need Family Support

Tara A. Trower

Tara A. Trower is an education reporter for the Austin American-Statesman *and currently resides in Austin, Texas. As a self-described air force brat, Trower grew up on military bases around the country. As one of the few African American students in her classes, she had contemplated dating interracially from an early age. In the following account Trower recalls her discussions with her father about her attraction to white boys in her youth, and she describes her hopes and fears many years later about bringing her white boyfriend home to meet her family.*

My father and I tackled the subject of interracial dating years before I was even allowed to date.

I was about 13 years old and watching Vanessa Huxtable's dating antics in the late 1980s on *The Cosby Show* [a popular sitcom about an affluent African American family], when I turned to my father and asked, "What would you do if I dated a white guy?"

His answer: "As long as he treats you right, I don't care what he looks like."

I had no particular boy in mind. But as an Air Force brat who had been stationed in such places as Minot, [North Dakota,] and Omaha, [Nebraska,] where my brother and I were one of a handful of African Americans at school, interracial dating seemed to be worth considering. The question was an innocent one, more revealing 18 years later than it was then.

After all, the man I intend to marry and brought home this summer to my parents is white.

Early Discouragements

The fact that I even considered as a child the prospect of dating outside my race is a testament to progress made in the years since my parents attended segregated public schools in Virginia, and the results on a personal level have been interesting—sometimes painful, sometimes blissful and often angst-ridden.

We moved to Austin during my freshman year. Adolescence is never easy—regardless of ethnicity. The boys I liked tended to be in my classes, and at Bowie High School in Southwest Austin those boys tended to be white. More than once I spilled my heart full of puppy love to one of my white male classmates, only to be told that I was a great girl, but his parents would kill him if he brought me home.

My father tried to protect me in his own way. He raised me to believe that I could accomplish anything if I worked hard enough. And I believed him.

When I was about 16 and an honors student, Dad awkwardly attempted once to explain the source of my romantic troubles. He said, "The way you talk will make black boys think you are stuck up, and white ones will not see you as attractive."

Harsh as it sounds (and crushing as it was to a teen psyche), I honestly believe he thought he was helping. His experience with interracial dating at Virginia Tech during the late 1960s–early '70s was his prism. Despite a few genuine relationships, others were tainted by having youthful rebellion as the goal, rather than mutual love and understanding. And most of those relationships in his experience were black men dating white women, not the reverse.

My First Experiences of Bringing a Boyfriend Home

During my college years in Chicago, I dated Aaron, an African American man from Atlanta. He was an engineer from a middle-class family. Race was a non-issue. The visits to my parents and my grandparents were laced only with the normal nervousness anyone has when bringing someone to meet their family for the first time: Will they like him, will there be awkward silences and will they embarrass me by asking about [having] kids?

The highlights of my college boyfriend's first visit to my parents' home: my father taking him aside to ask "What are your intentions?" and an unfortunate incident in which he crashed through my grandparents' ceiling while trying to stow a box in the attic for my grandmother. But that was all.

Aaron's and my conversations about how we would raise children started from the same basic belief: It is possible to be black and succeed in America, but we must be watchful in our endeavors because institutional and overt racism is still alive and well. We shared a common experience that was taken for granted. We knew what it was like to be black. The relationship had problems and that is why it ended, but race was never a factor.

A More Challenging Relationship

My current relationship of nearly two years with Dave has been far more complex. Friends and co-workers, black and white, asked questions early on: "Will your parents have a problem with it?" "Do your parents know he's white?" "Do his parents know you are black?"

I've spent far more time fretting about our racial differences than Dave has, trying to prepare him for the inevitability that someone will hurl a racial epithet or try to provoke him into a fight or the day when a cruel classmate calls our kid an "Oreo," or worse. I'm more likely than Dave to see racial disparities, and I'm more likely to empathize with others from a different ethnic background.

His parents, a university professor and a church secretary, taught him and his brothers the lesson of mutual respect for people, regardless of background—a lesson that has stuck.

Living in Austin means that interracial relationships are not quite the anomaly they are in other parts of the state. But occasionally someone will look at us strangely, and I will cringe inside and put myself on guard. We've discussed at length what it will mean to have biracial children and how to address issues of race and ethnicity with them.

While he has a good grasp of overt racism, his perception of institutional racism is much more limited. He admits that he has no idea what it is like to be followed in a department store, or trailed by cops while driving through [white suburban] West Lake Hills. It's a continuing dialogue, one that will continue long after we are married and have children.

A More Complicated Meeting

His family has welcomed me into the fold, without a pause or a stutterstep. The question of race hasn't really come up that much, except our ability to laugh when Dave's young niece announced that she wanted to be pretty and black like me.

But despite my father's straightforward answer to my question many years ago, the idea of Dave meeting my parents and bringing him to Virginia to meet my extended family made my stomach churn.

Over the years, a few of my female cousins have also dated white men. I overheard the conversations between my dad and my uncles, where the young men were viewed with far more suspicion than their black counterparts. There was more questioning of motives, so family dinners had the potential of feeling more like scientific observation.

Family Differences

And then there are the cultural differences. My grandmother still lives in the rural community where she was born, where whites, regardless of age, are still referred to as Mr. or Ms. so-and-so. She is the typical black matriarch: She runs the family and can be painfully direct. And there is no telling what she might say to a stranger. A test of loyalty is if you eat what she cooks, and Dave hates collard greens—one of her specialties.

And finally there is the issue of class. My grandparents were dirt poor. My grandmother got married before she was 16 and didn't learn how to read until her 50s. She held her family together though sheer willpower and lots of prayer. I have uncles who are executives for some of the nation's top companies. But one of my cousins has been shot, another is in jail for murder and an assortment of others have had children out of wedlock. My brother's roommate was gunned down and killed outside a convenience store down the street. All a far cry from Bowie High School, which Dave also attended. A far cry from the circles we mingle in here in Austin and our co-workers in the *Statesman* newsroom.

Finding Family Support

I should have given my family and Dave more credit. Our trip to Virginia in May was a good one. My father, true to his word, greeted Dave with open arms, complete with a trip to the golf course and late-night male bonding over the San Antonio Spurs. Dave tells me there was a serious discussion between the two of them about meeting my grandmother, where Dad tried to prep Dave for the possibility that Grandma Trower might say something quite politically incorrect.

The next day, we drove to my grandmother's modest house on Virginia's Eastern Shore. I think my grandmother hugged Dave no fewer than four times. And the only truly embarrassing question dealt with whether we were "shacking up." As she hugged me goodbye, she whispered in my ear, "Did I say too much?"

The sky didn't fall. There were no melodramatic moments. In fact, my mother wrote me later to say that Dave reminds her in some ways of my father as a younger man.

Unknown to me at the time, during that trip Dave asked my father for permission to marry me. Dad gladly gave it and welcomed him to the family. Dave proposed [in July 2005] on the balcony of the Stephen F. Austin Hotel, and we plan to be married in April [2006].

A Supportive Family Is Critical for Interracial Couples

A few months before the visit, I rented the original *Guess Who's Coming to Dinner* [a 1967 film dealing with the issue of interracial romance], a movie I had not seen since I was a child. I am struck by how many of the concerns raised in the movie about interracial relationships are still valid. [African American actor] Sidney Poitier's character tells his fiancee's parents that he knows the couple will face many tribulations, but having the blessing of the family is critical and without it he will call the whole thing off.

Progress when it comes to race relations in America is relative, and I'm not naive enough to believe that love conquers all. But I'm thankful and blessed there's at least one battle Dave and I don't have to fight, and we'll have the reinforcement of family to fight the rest.

SOCIAL ISSUES
FIRSTHAND

CHAPTER 3

Interracial Families

Tracing the Black Roots of My Biracial Identity

Zoë Welsh

Zoë Welsh, the biracial daughter of English and Jamaican parents, resides in England and works as a television producer for the British Broadcasting Corporation. Raised by her white mother and maternal grandmother after her father left the family when she was nine months old, she has wrestled most of her life with the question of her identity. Until she took a life-changing trip to Jamaica, she was never able to decide if she was white, black, or brown.

In the account that follows, Welsh describes what it was like for her to travel to a place where for the first time most of the people looked like her. She had never before felt so at home in a foreign land.

Discovering that she had a loving family and a place to call home in Jamaica impacted Welsh more than she had anticipated. Returning to England, she felt as if she was finally complete, able to understand and accept the black side of her identity as she had accepted her whiteness, and to be proud of the richness that both sides of her family offered.

It was a journey that I think I always knew I would make. A journey that in the end, I knew I would have to make, to a destination I feared I might never reach. You see for me, this was more than a journey. This was a search to find the answer to a question I'd been asking myself my entire life.

Am I black? I guess you shouldn't have to ask yourself that question, but when you've been brought up by a white mum and white maternal grandmother, it's a question brought into sharp focus as you realise the childish taunts in the playground are directed at you.

Questioning My Identity

You see, I used to actually have to ask myself the question, "*Am I black?*" I was just nine months old when my Dad left my Mum. Too young to notice my obvious difference and too young to miss him . . . at first. But, where do you look for your racial identity when you're a different colour to your parents? I looked wherever I found people who looked like me! My Mum recounts a particularly embarrassing experience when, at the age of two I pointed and shouted 'daddy' at an unsuspecting black conductor on the local bus. My outburst may have been something to do with the fact he was one of only a handful of West Indians living in Milton Keynes [a city in southeast England] in the early 1970s. In my linear toddler's mind he looked something like the black man grinning from the photograph given pride of place on Mum's G-Plan [popular English furniture brand] coffee table.

The realisation that I was different might have kicked in early, but I didn't start to intellectualise the difference until my blackness was pointed out to me, until racism forced me to. It's more than thirty years since I first started to question my identity. I am now a television producer; I have a good life, great friends, nice home, new car and take the requisite long haul holidays each year! But there's always been a huge void in my life. I've never quite been able to get my head around the "Who am I?" question, the "Am I white, black, or brown?" Wherever I am on my perception of the racial colour chart, I've internalised the confusion my entire life, or I had until quite recently.

A Life-Changing Journey

I can't explain why I felt ready to finally search out the answer to my question, I just did. I had the time, I had some money and most importantly I had the courage I needed to set off on a trip that I knew would change my life forever. I just didn't know by how much.

In May [2004], just two days after my thirty-sixth birthday, I flew to Jamaica, to meet up with my father, a man I had met just four times in my life, and a family I had never met. A family I knew nothing about and who lived a life I could only just begin to imagine. As my Air Jamaica flight to Kingston taxied along the runway in preparation for takeoff, my gut was twisted with anxiety, fear and excitement, and once again I asked myself the question, "Am I black?" I also asked myself "Would I belong?" "Would I be too white to be black, too British to be Jamaican?"

When I finally stepped on Jamaican soil for the first time, clichéd though this might sound, I truly felt I'd come home. As I walked through arrivals and passport control I looked around and saw people, black people, brown people, not many white people, people like me! I felt quite unlike I'd ever felt on any of my other travels and nothing like a tourist. I had a huge urge as the immigration officer stamped my passport to say, "Do you know, I'm half Jamaican?!" Ridiculous, as if he'd be interested! But I couldn't believe it, for the first time in my life I was able to think the words and not feel inadequate, or somehow an impostor.

Meeting My Jamaican Family

The next few weeks were nothing short of a full-on emotional roller coaster. A whirlwind of experience that scooped me up, dragged me along and spewed me out a completely different person at the end of it! There were major highs and major lows. Sadly, most of the lows had to do with my father and my relationship with him. I knew from the outset that I didn't really want a Dad. It felt too late for that somehow, but as a grown woman I would have liked to have found a friend. Someone to get to know, someone to guide me, someone to encourage and support me and in return someone that I could grow to respect and love. But in the end the thirty-six year separation was a chasm just too wide to bridge. I may not have found what I was looking for in my father, but in my new Aunt and Uncle, I found far much more. . . .

There were so many highs. My first trip into the Blue Mountains to see for myself where Dad and his family are from is an experience I will hold in my heart forever. As I sat in the congregation at Mount Fletcher Methodist Church, a small, whitewashed building nestled deep in the plush, lush, fragrant Blue Mountains, I struggled to contain my tears. I thought of and tried to imagine the generations of Welshes who had sat on the same church pew. How different might my life have been had I been born and raised in Jamaica? How might I have taken for granted the beauty that now rendered me speechless? They were questions without answers, but ones that went round and round in my head regardless. After the service, as I stumbled through the graveyard, I found my Dad's Mum's tomb, but still I didn't cry. I wanted to cry though, for the Grandmother I had never known, a face I couldn't picture and a voice I had never heard. I felt more than sad, I felt cheated. The tears finally came later, as I was taken even further into the mountains and to Great Aunt Daisy's house. As the ninety-three year old matriarch realised who I was, she praised the Lord, and then praised him again and again, and I did too! I felt part of the family, part of something much bigger, something with a past, a real present and a graspable future. At last I felt I belonged somewhere.

At Home in a New Land

Much to the amusement of the family, I spent most of my trip morphing into a kid in a toy shop. It was just all too much, too exciting, too different! My first jelly coconut, macheted especially for me, tasted nothing like the dried up desiccated stuff I remembered from home ec. classes! Being able to pick ripe juicy mangoes straight from the tree, chewing on sugar cane, all new to me, but everyday stuff to my folks! I loved the food, the rice and peas, the fish, the bammy [flat bread made from grated cassava], even the festival! As I lost myself in the lyricism of the Patois [Jamaican creole language, a vernacular form of English], I grew fascinated by its rhythm and pace, not bad for someone who for much of the time didn't understand a word of it! There were so many 'pinch me I'm dreaming' moments. From the overproof rum I shared with the village undertaker at Cousin Eddie's rum shop, cum [with] garage, cum Sunday night sound system to mesmerising hours spent three thousand feet up in the Blue Mountains watching the sun go down and night descend on Jamaica's capital below.

On a more profound level I loved the fact that I could be me. I didn't stand out, unless the enthusiasm for my new found homeland dulled my senses! No one batted an eyelid at the strangely accented mixed-race woman, with her big hair and ever-widening smile! Since returning home, I've pondered the whole nature/nurture argument more than ever before. For the first thirty-six years of my life, I've been a mixed-race woman, living a life surrounded by white family and friends and embracing, thanks to not having the choice otherwise, the white side of me. Now for the first time in my life, I have a completeness I could have only dreamed of a few months ago. I know now that regardless of my access to it, my Jamaican self has always been there, albeit lying dormant and denied. Nature has finally been able to show its strength!

Completed by a Family I Had Only Dreamed About

And what about now? Well, I have a new second home and a huge extended family, something as an only child, I have only ever been able to dream about. I have cousins, second cousins, great Aunts, a wonderful Aunt, and the most amazing Uncle a girl could ask for! During my time in Jamaica I developed a swelling pride for a country and people whom I came to feel part of. Finally I was able to answer my question, "Am I black?"

The answer? Who cares? You see, I'm me. Clichéd? Perhaps? But it's enough of an answer for me. I am Zoë first and foremost. I have a white English Mum and a black Jamaican Dad and I now know where they are both from. I can visualise their lives and piece together the jigsaw that makes them the people they are. In completing their jigsaw, I've finally found the missing piece of mine. I no longer feel the need to label myself; if others do, that's their business! I'm happy to be mixed and I'm happy to be me. I am lucky to have two homes to call my own; my familiar UK one and the unfolding magical mystery that is Jamaica.

At last I can be happy; happy in my own skin, my brown skin, and proud of it. I am comfortable in the knowledge of what's gone into making me, and I'm bursting with excitement, anticipation and hopes and dreams for the new experiences I know will play a part in forming the rest of my life. I had known even before I boarded [Flight] JM002 that my journey would lead me to a different me, but do I like the new me? Too right I do. I feel free, liberated, and at ease with life. Who could ask for more?

Parents Need to Talk About Race with Their Mixed-Heritage Children

Jen Chau

Jen Chau, born to Jewish and Chinese parents, is a professional speaker, writer, community organizer, and activist on multiracial issues. She is the founder of Swirl, Inc., an organization dedicated to serving and empowering the mixed-race community, and she is also the codirector of New/Demographic and Mixed Media Watch.

When she was a child, Chau recalls being questioned by other children about her racial identity. Her skin was much darker than her mother's, leading some people to assume that they were not related. These incidents were painful for Chau, and she became self-conscious about her identity, always trying to anticipate how others would perceive her. She did not discuss these issues openly with her parents, however; to her they seemed inappropriate to bring up.

In the essay that follows, Chau reflects on her experiences and encourages parents to talk openly with their mixed-race children about race, identity, and racism. She advocates this because not all children will let their parents know how they really feel or what they really are experiencing.

It's July in New York City, and it's hot. You would think that the high temperatures would keep people in the air-conditioned indoors or at least drive them away to the beaches, but the streets still sizzle with people. Everyone has a water bottle, an ice cream cone, or a fan in hand. Summer is definitely here.

You can't walk in Manhattan without seeing at least a few mixed families on every block. Mixed families are not new, but it definitely seems that they are appearing with more and more frequency. Now that school is out, the streets are flooded with little ones in carriages, kids running alongside their parents, or babies bopping to every step as parents give rides on hot shoulders.

I notice these families not only because of the work that I do, but also because I wonder how different it is today for them than it was for my family. Do they openly talk about race and identity? Or are these issues brushed under the rug and neatly taken care of with a phrase like, "But honey, you have the best of both worlds?" My hope is that there is more conversation today considering the growing numbers of mixed families and the wealth of resources available to them. Due to these two circumstances, there is definitely a greater awareness of mixed identity than there was in the early 80s. There is no longer an excuse to leave such issues of identity unaddressed.

Standing Out

Just 20 years ago, I was in elementary school—excited to put my books away and ready for a season of swimming pools, bathing suits and sibling rivalry. My family (complete with mom, grandparents and two younger brothers—dad worked during the summers) would head off to our club in Long Beach a few times a week to soak in the sun, play, and relax. We kids never went to camp and never really wanted to.

There were kids around for us to play with, but it was always a homogeneous crowd. The other families were all pretty much white and middle class. Then there was my family. I don't know if my mother still received such comments when we were older, but she was always asked how long she had been my baby-sitter as she toted me around in a carriage through parks in our neighborhood. Clearly, this olive-skinned baby could not be hers.

My brothers and I spent most of the day splashing around in the pool, playing basketball, and fighting as most siblings do. We hardly had time to notice race. However, this does not mean that it never came up. I remember the questions that would usually come specifically to me. In a sea of kids who were pale or bright pink with sunburn, my brothers and I would get pretty tan. I mean, we were in the sun constantly. I remember a little girl who stood on the top step of the pool right alongside me one day. We both swirled our big toes around in the water tentatively. We were squinting because the sun reflected off of the crystal ripples and bounced back at our faces. And then she turned to me, and with a whisper, said, "Are you black?"

I don't remember what I said, but I do remember the feeling of surprise. Is this girl that oblivious that she could think that this Jewish and Chinese girl is black? Or was she just more open-minded to think that I could be considered to fit into this community? But the whisper . . . Did she think that she was blowing a cover that I was trying to keep? Did she think that I would be embarrassed to be asked? Or was she already tuned in to the taboo of discussing race in this blunt manner? This brief interaction made me realize a couple of things.

Fitting In

First, it made me think about groups and exactly where I fit in. Here at this young age, I already knew that the communities in which I was "supposed" to belong were not necessarily so willing to embrace me; others were. So much of it had to do with the way I looked. I knew this because so many people made assumptions about me and who I was, based on first glance. The same girl might have thought that I was Hawai'ian if I had only been wearing my shell necklace that day (this would also happen to me frequently). It made me realize how fluid identity was. Even though we were taught in school that there were five racial categories (and nothing more), I realized that things were not as simple as that. I knew that I didn't fit into just one box, and the fact that people thought of me in such varying and contrasting terms merely confirmed that notion.

The second realization was that I would probably have to deal with this type of question for a long time. Very often people in school or at the park would ask me about my "background." I was familiar with the questions, and with people trying to figure me out. I was also growing accustomed to the feeling of others identifying me in a way that might be completely different from how I would identify myself. Situations like this felt complicated and I remember trying to understand what people saw when they looked at me. I aimed to see what they saw. There became this constant focus on what others thought about me and saw in me. Because there weren't other kids around me who were also mixed, I didn't have any other examples to look to, other people to model myself after, or big sibling types to look to for advice. I didn't really have the opportunity to develop my thoughts and feelings about my own identity—I mainly worked to make other people comfortable with me as a means of fitting in.

When to Talk

Just recently, I attended a talk in my capacity as the Executive Director of Swirl, Inc. Swirl is an anti-racist, grassroots organization that serves the mixed heritage community. I founded this non-profit almost 5 years ago in order to create a space for mixed individuals, couples, and families. So, here I was, sitting on a panel that was about mixed identity and parenting mixed children, when one audience member made a comment that troubled me. She said "Well, I know that my son doesn't have any issues regarding his mixed identity." I asked her, "How do you know?" She replied, "He never says anything."

As we all know, kids don't always talk about everything that is really on their minds. I for one, kept a lot of things to myself because I thought that most of the harassment I was getting, at Hebrew School for example, was my fault. I was ashamed of my difference and didn't think that the fact that I was constantly teased about my Chinese heritage would be acceptable dinner table conversation. I kept a lot of things to myself and dealt with things much later on as an adult. Obviously, this is not ideal. I suggested that this parent really take the time to ask her son about his experiences in school, with his friends, with his teachers, etc. Kids are hyper-sensitive to things that we may not realize they are even aware of, and rather than thinking that silence means everything is okay, we should be trained to ask and then listen. Providing a forum for these kinds of difficult topics is extremely crucial. I know that I would have benefited from having this kind of space to talk about how it felt to be a mixed girl.

Now it's quite possible that this woman's son indeed has no "issues." But why is it that we have been socialized to care and act only when there is something wrong? If there are no "issues," shouldn't we want to know what's happening in our children's lives anyway? Experiences (especially the positive ones!) should be discussed and processed. It is so important for children to be nurtured and given attention as they develop their identities.

Exposure to Diversity Is Not Enough

The other piece of this is that this mother felt that there should be no issues because her child is constantly around other kids of color (including mixed kids) at school and in their community. Also, she felt that she had done the work necessary to prepare herself for raising a mixed child of color. I have talked to many parents just like her who feel that race is a conversation that has been done to death. "We aren't going to focus on the negative, we will *celebrate* difference!"

While celebration is great, having parties for the Lunar New Year, St. Patrick's, Kwanzaa [a holiday celebrating African American heritage] and El Dia De Los Muertos [Day of the Dead, a traditional Mexican holiday] in your home will not exempt your children from having to navigate difficult situations regarding ethnicity. The fact that you build a sanctuary of understanding and peace in your house doesn't mean that your child is going to avoid racism once he leaves your front door. Exposure to diversity is definitely a good step in the right direction, but it's not the only step you need to take.

It's also important to realize that when we talk about mixed race identity, we are having a conversation about race that hasn't really been had *enough* yet. I have attended many race conferences that neglect to even address the mixed heritage angle, or they merely include the topic by having one workshop out of hundreds. In many ways, mixed identity is not yet a real part of our national consciousness. This should further push parents to talk with their mixed children, since it is highly probable that children aren't having discussions about mixed identity in school or anywhere else. It's difficult when kids do not see themselves reflected in the outside world (television, movies, etc.). It's important that they are fully recognized at home by family members.

Sending Our Mixed-Race Son to Chinese Culture School

Gish Jen

In the narrative that follows, Gish Jen, a Chinese writer and college professor who resides in Cambridge, Massachusetts, describes her and her Irish husband's struggle with the decision to send their son to Chinese culture school against the child's wishes. Although she and her husband want to raise their son to appreciate and embrace all facets of his heritage, they decided that he should first learn more about Chinese culture after he denies that aspect of his background in a confrontation with several neighborhood children. Jen believes that in a society in which a person may label and reject a person merely on the basis of his or her physical appearance, her son should be taught to value his heritage. Once he is older, she reasons, he can be taught to define himself without regard to race.

That my son, Luke, age four, goes to Chinese-culture school seems inevitable to most people, even though his father is of Irish descent. For certain ethnicities trump others; Chinese, for example, trumps Irish. This has something to do with the relative distance of certain cultures from mainstream American culture, but it also has to do with race. For as we all know, it is not only certain ethnicities that trump others but certain colors: black trumps white, for example, always and forever; a mulatto is not a kind of white person, but a kind of black person.

And so it is, too, that my son is considered a kind of Asian person whose manifest destiny is to embrace Asian things.

The Chinese language. Chinese food. Chinese New Year. No one cares whether he speaks Gaelic or wears green on

Saint Patrick's Day. For though Luke's skin is fair, and his features mixed, people see his straight black hair and "know" who he is.

An Unwelcome Identity

But is this how we should define ourselves, by other people's perceptions? My husband, Dave, and I had originally hoped for Luke to grow up embracing his whole complex ethnic heritage. We had hoped to pass on to him values and habits of mind that had actually survived in both of us.

Then one day, Luke combed his black hair and said he was turning it yellow. Another day, a fellow mother reported that her son had invited all blond-haired children like himself to his birthday party. And yet another day, Luke was happily scooting around the Cambridge Common playground when a pair of older boys, apparently brothers, blocked his way. "You're Chinese!" they shouted, leaning on the hood of Luke's scooter car. "You are! You're Chinese!" So brazen were these kids that even when I, an adult, intervened, they continued to shout. Luke answered, "No, I'm not!"—to no avail; it was not clear if the boys even heard him. Then the boys' mother called to them from some distance away, outside the fence, and though her voice was no louder than Luke's, they left obediently.

Behind them opened a great, rippling quiet, like the wash of a battleship.

Unsatisfactory Advice

Luke and I immediately went over things he could say if anything like that ever happened again. I told him that he was 100 percent American, even though I knew from my own childhood in Yonkers that these words would be met only with derision. It was a sorry chore. Since then, I have not asked him about the incident, hoping he has forgotten about it, and wishing that I could, too. For I wish I could forget the sight of those kids' fingers on the hood of Luke's little car. I wish I could forget their loud attack, but also Luke's soft defense: No, I'm not.

An Uncomfortable Decision

Chinese-culture school. After dozens of phone calls, I was elated to discover the Greater Boston Chinese Cultural Association nearby in West Newton. The school takes children at three, has a wonderful sense of community, and is housed in a center paid for, in part, by great karaoke fund-raising events. . . . There are even vendors who bring home-style Chinese food to sell after class—stuff you can't get in a restaurant. Dave and I couldn't wait for the second class, and a chance to buy more bao [Chinese buns] for our freezer.

But in the car on the way to the second class, Luke announced that he didn't want to go to Chinese school anymore. He said that the teacher talked mostly about ducks and bears and that he wasn't interested in ducks and bears. And I knew this was true. I knew that Luke was interested only in whales and ships. And what's more, I knew we wouldn't push him to take swimming lessons if he didn't want to, or music. Chinese school was a wonderful thing, but there was a way in which we were accepting it as somehow nonoptional. Was that right? Hadn't we always said that we didn't want our son to see himself as more essentially Chinese than Irish?

Yet we didn't want him to deny his Chinese heritage, either. And if there were going to be incidents on the playground, we wanted him to know what *Chinese* meant. So when Luke said again that he didn't really want to go to Chinese school, I said, "Oh, really?" Later on, we could try to teach him to define himself irrespective of race. For now, though, he was going to Chinese school. I exchanged glances with Dave. And then together, in a most carefully casual manner, we squinted at the road and kept going.

The New Traditional Family

Stewart David Ikeda

Stewart David Ikeda is a self-described hapa (the Hawaiian term for "half" and connoting mixed race) writer and lecturer on multicultural issues. His novel What the Scarecrow Said, *an epic story about the experiences of a Japanese American family during World War II, was nominated for the Pulitzer Prize. Ikeda has taught literature courses at several universities and is currently involved in a number of media projects, including IM-Diversity, Inc., a multicultural publishing company.*

As he describes in the following essay, the adoption of a Guatemalan infant by his Japanese aunt and Caucasian uncle moved him to reflect on the changing nature of the Japanese American family. Ikeda realized that this mix of racial and cultural currents in his aunt and uncle's family was reflective of modern Japanese American culture as a whole, as interracial marriages lead to more and more mixed-race children. At the same time, Japanese tradition and Japanese American history, diluted and ignored for several decades after World War II, is consciously being reclaimed by many third- and fourth-generation Japanese American families. In many ways, Ikeda reflects, the nature of the Japanese family has been changed irrevocably by the American experience, but the resurgence of Japanese traditions and interest in the Japanese American experience reveals that that heritage will not be forgotten.

When I first saw her in Arizona that Christmas of 1993, she was sleeping in my grandparents' room. I tiptoed inside and waited until my eyes adjusted to the dark. A faint whispering noise made it sound as if she had a cold. Squinting, I could barely make out her cheeks raising and lowering with small breaths. Yet, I immediately recognized her as one of us.

Stewart David Ikeda, "Adoption, Hapas, and Asian-American Heritage," *Pacific Citizen*, December 2001. Reproduced by permission IMDiversity.com.

I don't mean that I accepted her, despite her newness, her foreign origins, her racial distinctiveness. Nor do I believe that it was simply a mystical or chemical or emotional bonding between an innocent and an adult who had eagerly anticipated her coming, though that force was strong. And I don't even think it was how her arrival eased the ache of my grandfather's death in this very room not long before. Rather, I mean that I experienced an instantaneous sense that my new cousin—born in Guatemala, adopted by my sansei [third-generation Japanese American] aunt and hakujin [white] uncle that bittersweet Thanksgiving—already belonged.

A Hapa like Me

Even before I parted the curtains to view her features in the morning light, the baby had exhibited a distinctly Ikeda-like stoicism. Formative months in a clean but understaffed orphanage gave her an uncommon patience in both solitude and company. She had not cried upon waking, but amused herself with a kind of soft crib-singing for some time until we noticed her. She did not protest being picked up by a stranger in a strange, dark room. Nor did she panic when her parents did not appear for over an hour, having taken advantage of the many willing baby-sitters to take a rare outing together.

We quietly sized each other up. She tested the foreign bristles of my beard and mustache with her fingertips. They were warm and a bit moist, and it made me feel overly hairy and brutish. And for my part, I marveled at the light-tanned complexion of her round face, the straight, just-short-of-black bangs, the slightly folded lids that spoke to her part-native origins. Mariana appeared for all the world to be the biological offspring of her new adoptive parents. In short, a hapa, like me.

Losing and Recovering Our Identities

Since then, I've had more experience and occasion to reflect on the little yonsei [fourth-generation Japanese American] from Guatemala, and what she means to me both personally and for what I envision for Japanese America in the 21st century. It is a commonplace that JAs [Japanese Americans] overall have been "diluted" in the limited blood-quantum statistical sense, evidenced in our high out-marriage [marrying non-Japanese] rate and, most concretely, in our younger generations' mixed-race bodies. It is somewhat less common to observe that our collective wartime upheaval and subsequent hyperassimilation have left even our "pure" yonsei, with two sansei parents, "culturally diluted," too. As a diasporic people—like the Jews, forcefully dispersed, wandering, surviving in our separate ways—we face a mounting struggle to maintain our distinctiveness, stories, and heritage.

On a national book tour a few years ago, I was fortunate to speak with hundreds of nisei [second-generation Japanese Americans]. I recall one at each stop (usually a woman my grandmother's age) struggling to the podium under five or six copies of my hardback book. She gripped my arm fiercely while I personalized each one for a different grandchild who "doesn't know anything about our side of the family, isn't interested in it, and isn't Japanese at all. How did you get interested in this?" she wanted to know. Ironically, sansei and yonsei always asked, "How did you find out about this?"

A long-standing generational communications gap had created a kind of cultural amnesia among JAs. Mainland nisei had spent so many years not talking about their lives, distancing themselves from things Japanese, forgetting what their parents had taught them. Meanwhile, grandchildren living scattered in mostly-white neighborhoods across the country, thousands of miles from the nearest J-town [Japantown neighborhood] had little opportunity to form a sense of JA cultural identity. Later, after redress [apology and monetary compensation by the U.S. government for the involuntary internment of Japanese Americans during World War II], when grandparents were ready to answer questions about the family history, the grandchildren had too little background exposure or knowledge to know what questions to ask.

"Thank you for writing about this," that nisei lady would whisper. Full of anxiety, even panic, she wanted desperately to know what will be left of our Japanese heritage in the near future and seemed to fear a kind of extinction. I was not the first author to write about immigration, exclusion, internment, and assimilation, and certainly not the best. But I think what she meant was that the handful of then-young hapa writers like me who had chosen to explore Japanese-American lives in print created some hope that her own family's interest would also be there before it was too late. What she was really saying, I think, was, thank you for not letting "our family" disappear.

Unexpected Forms of Family and Culture

I believe that a distinct Japanese-American culture can and will survive, but perhaps—as Mariana's Guatemalan origins and place as an Ikeda suggest—in an unexpected form. It will be preserved only very purposefully as family heritage, not automatically as a geographic accident, racial legacy, or birthright. There may be more of us in this century who don't in fact "look Japanese" or speak Japanese than those who do. If most JAs will look like Mariana and me, we must accept that the JA experience is inherently multicultural and changing—something different from our Japanese roots that we are making up as we go along.

When she was a baby, it was easy for the other hapa cousins to project onto Mariana those Japanese-y traits that connected her more closely to ourselves. Changing her diapers, my cousin and I scrutinized slight dark areas at her lower back and decided they were "Mongolian spots." In writing and conversation, I have always truncated her name, lending its sound a pronunciation after the fashion of the Japanese Mariko, the name of a great-aunt.

At the same time, we were conscious of her unique origins. My cousin Gillian, who had studied Spanish in school, played clapping games with Mari in that language. My aunt and uncle made the larger adjustment of moving from their generally homogeneous East Coast suburb to a more multicultural neighborhood in a diverse Arizona school district. As a consequence, Mari may ultimately learn Spanish despite her family's linguistic deficiencies. A good thing, and not only because of her roots. Like me, she will continuously be greeted and questioned on the street by Hispanics who presume her Spanish fluency based on her appearance. Like me, she may also be taken for Middle Eastern, Mediterranean, perhaps Turk, and will elicit surprise to explain that her maternal family is Japanese.

Consciousness of Roots

In any case, she already has a nascent sense of what sets her apart from her mainstream peers. Like her cousins, "she knows she's different in some way from the blonde, blue-eyed kids in school," her father says. But, asked if she has a conscious sense of herself as the daughter of a multicultural, multiracial, and ethnically Japanese family, he confesses, "I don't know. She's a kid, you know? She's like a sponge and just takes everything in and processes it somehow," often without a lot of discussion.

Also like her cousins, she will have a consciousness of her immigrant roots. For one thing, Mari's parents determined early on to disclose the story of her adoption. Further, she has seen the arranged marriage photos of her great-grandparents, heard the stories of their pioneering emigration from Japan, played with katakana [Japanese character] language cards, studied the hanging scrolls, tasted the cuisine, and lived with what heirlooms remain to our family.

But beneath these surfaces—physical appearance, and cultural trappings like sushi and ikebana [flower arranging]—I wonder about Mari's emotional and psychic sense of self as she ages. Will she, too, feel a particular comfort among Japanese and East Asian Americans? Will she desire to travel to Japan to visit our family's villages, admire JA role models, fantasize about living in Hawaii as a mythical place populated by a majority of people "like us"? Will she date Asian Americans? Or, will the story of her birth and racial roots pull her more forcefully? Will she study Spanish and be able to navigate Guatemala should she choose to visit the land of her birth parents, or Japanese so that she can converse with visiting relatives? Or both, or neither? And how much does it matter?

New Traditional Families

Such reflection arises this time every year as I recall the anniversary of her arrival. Further, I am one of those cursed relatives who selects kids' gifts based on what's good for them—educational and empowering. I frequent multicultural toy and book businesses, but when it comes down to it, I never know what to buy. An Asian doll or a South American? This year, I'm weighing Yoshiko Uchida's *The Bracelet*, about a little girl's internment, against *1621*, a book about Thanksgiving from the historical perspective of Wampanoag Indians. Sometimes I tie myself in knots and ultimately settle for a book about Hanukkah or a crafts kit.

I can be accused of over-thinking and perhaps inappropriately politicizing these decisions for a little girl who would herself probably opt for anything featuring Harry Potter. But don't we all want our kids to see themselves positively reflected in the world around them, to be proud of their heritage and full of self-esteem, and to learn about other cultures and perspectives?

I've been thinking about this, too, because in the past few years, two sansei relatives and another family friend have all adopted children, as it happens, from China. As it also happens, all are in interracial relationships. These children will look superficially more like their mothers, and thus like a "traditional" JA family. They will also stand out in any gathering of their much more numerous hapa cousins.

The longer I think about our "non-traditional" family, it begins to seem in fact very traditional in ways that matter. In hours of conversation with my friend Frances Wang, a Chinese-American writer and my colleague on Asian-American Village Online, I have come to think that in general, Asian conceptions of family may be fundamentally different from those of other U.S. ethnic groups. For example, given my grandfather's eight siblings, the Ikeda clan is large and diverse, and the relationships so complicated that at reunions, everyone is either "auntie," "uncle," or "cousin." Among more traditional nisei, at least, families-by-marriage are families, period; I never heard the distinction "in-laws" spoken by Ikedas, which is unlike my WASP [white Anglo-Saxon Protestant] maternal side. A number of non-blood-related folks across the century have been designated auntie and uncle because of our families' closeness based on original Japanese prefectures. Add to this the unnatural closeness of non-related nisei who had been thrust together in new artificial "families" in camp, relocation, and the army, and the definition of "kin" becomes trickier still. And finally, I have always been made to understand that should I ever get to visit Japan, there was a network of far-distant relations that was eager and duty-bound to take me under their wings pretty much for however long I desired—and vice-versa. Suddenly, the notion of extended family becomes international in scope.

We Are All Hapas Now

There is a line of thinking that suggests we are all—all of us twenty-first-century Americans of every background—psychically and culturally hapa. Globalization plus our increasing diversity have rendered us cultural, if not racial hybrids. Maybe Mari will conceive of herself as just another multicultural, individual American.

How much can a kid really understand or care about such things? In the year-round Arizona sun, Mari's skin has darkened, and her mother believes this will prove increasingly significant to her sense of self as she ages. But at the same time, she has given kimono demonstrations with Grandma to her Brownie troop; last time we were together, we practiced eating with hashi [chopsticks] together. Mari knows Grandma is Japanese, but seems not to recognize her mom in that category. Asked what she is herself, Mari admits she doesn't know . . . yet.

It takes time, maturity, and wisdom for us to grow into our skins. Some of us never do. I understand Mari's hesitancy because, as I've written elsewhere and at other times, . . . I too had to "learn to be a Japanese American" after being born— like Mariana—something else. I chose it, worked at it, and my family was my teacher. We're teaching Mariana about our heritage, and Mariana in turn is teaching me something about the difference between culture and race, between heritage and blood. I am reminded of this every Christmas, when I recall the great gift the Ikedas received in 1993, the huge new love we shared as a family. And what could be more "traditional" than that?

Organizations to Contact

Association of Multiethnic Americans (AMEA)
PO Box 29223, Los Angeles, CA   90029-0223
Web site: www.ameasite.org

AMEA is an international association of organizations dedicated to advocacy, education, and collaboration on behalf of the multiethnic, multiracial, and transracial adoption community. AMEA provides access to culturally competent resources by connecting service providers to clients; facilitates collaboration between organizations dedicated to multiethnic, multiracial, and transracial adoptee issues; and conducts needs-assessments to identify and meet unmet needs and recognize new trends. The AMEA Web site features essays, education resources, book reviews, and links to related Web sites and organizations.

Biracial Family Network (BFN)
PO Box 2387, Chicago, IL   60690-2387
(773) 288-3644
e-mail: bfnchicago@yahoo.com
Web site: http://users.arczip.com/xmen3/bfnchicago

The Biracial Family Network is a nonprofit public benefit corporation organized to help eliminate prejudice and discrimination. It assists individuals and families of diverse ethnic ancestry to improve the quality of their intercultural relationships via education and social activities. BFN works to establish spaces of comfort and connection among members of multiracial families, to take action against racist and discriminatory practices, and to educate people and communities about multiracial experiences. BFN offers a Student Research Program, which is designed to give students access to their organization and certain resources to aid them in the completion of their projects.

FUSION: A Program for Mixed Heritage Youth

3607 Kansas St., Oakland, CA   94619
e-mail: info@fusionprogram.org
Web site: www.fusionprogram.org

The FUSION Program for Mixed Heritage Youth seeks to support multiracial, multiethnic, and/or transracially adoptive youth and their families. Fusion offers yearly summer camps for mixed-heritage students aged seven through twelve and employs interested and qualified high school students as junior camp counselors. The FUSION Web site contains an extensive list of books, Internet sites, and organizations related to interracial issues.

IMDiversity, Inc.

140 Carondelet St., New Orleans, LA   70130
(832) 615-8871
Web site: www.imdiversity.com

IMDiversity, Inc. is dedicated to providing career and self-development information to all minorities, specifically African Americans, Asian Americans, Hispanic Americans, Native Americans, and women. In addition to providing access to a large database of equal opportunity employers committed to workplace diversity, the IMDiversity site offers articles on news and topics of interest to the multiracial community.

Interracial Family Circle (IFC)

923 E. Chalk Point Rd., West River, MD   20778
(301) 261-9066
e-mail: info@interracialfamilycircle.org
Web site: www.interracialfamilycircle.org

The Interracial Family Circle provides opportunities for the education, support, and socialization of multiracial individuals, families, people involved in interracial relationships, and transracial adoptive families in the Washington, D.C., metropolitan area. IFC holds roundtable discussions, public forums, and living room chats about issues of importance to multiracial families and orchestrates annual family-friendly Martin Luther King Day celebrations. In addition to the above activities, IFC publishes a newsletter on multiracial issues and offers resources for adults and children on its Web site.

Interracial Voice
Web site: www.webcom.com/~intvoice

Interracial Voice is an independent, information-oriented, networking news journal, serving the mixed-race/interracial community in cyberspace. This electronic publication advocates universal recognition of mixed-race individuals as constituting a separate racial entity and supported the initiative to establish a multiracial category on the 2000 Census. The Interracial Voice Web site publishes essays, interviews, news items, letters, and poetry on interracial issues and hosts a discussion forum for members.

INTERracialWeb.com
Web site: http://magazine.interracialweb.com

INTERracialWeb.com is a magazine and blog site serving the interracial community. The site features articles, essays, quizzes, news items, and products, and offers various services and volunteer opportunities to members.

MAVIN Foundation
600 First Ave., Suite 600, Seattle, Washington   98104
(206) 622-7101 • fax: (206) 622-2231
e-mail: info@mavinfoundation.org
Web site: www.mavin.net

MAVIN Foundation is committed to creating a society that recognizes the complexity of race, racism, and identity. MAVIN Foundation projects explore the experiences of mixed-heritage people, transracial adoptees, and interracial relationships, and offer support to multiracial families and students. Through its site it provides numerous resources for multiracial individuals, including a parenting resource titled *Multiracial Child Resource Book*.

Mixed Media Watch
Web site: www.mixedmediawatch.com

Mixed Media Watch is a Web log that monitors representations of mixed people, couples, families, and transracial adoptees in film, television, radio, and print media. The site features articles and opinion pieces on celebrities, affirmative action, hate crimes, interracial relationships, racial passing, movies, and other topics, particularly as they are related to media depictions of interracial individuals and families.

The Multiracial Activist (TMA)
PO Box 8208, Alexandria, VA   22306-8208
(703) 593-2065 • fax: 760-875-8547
Web site: www.multiracial.com

The Multiracial Activist is a libertarian activist journal covering social and civil liberties issues of interest to biracial or multiracial individuals, interracial couples/families, and transracial adoptees. In addition to an online journal, TMA publishes a Web log and a monthly newsletter. It also supports an online forum.

Multiracial Families Program
Hiawatha Branch YMCA, Minneapolis, MN   55406
(612) 729-7397

The Multiracial Families Program has more than nine hundred families on its mailing list and has been in existence for more than thirteen years. The program hosts support groups, social activities, and workshops throughout the year, in addition to an annual event, the Multiracial Family Conference and Celebration.

Pact—An Adoption Alliance
4179 Piedmont Ave., Suite 330, Oakland, CA   94611
(510) 243-9460 • fax: (510) 243-9970
e-mail: info@pactadopt.org
Web site: www.pactadopt.org

Pact is a nonprofit membership organization offering lifelong support to all members in families of color touched by adoption. Pact's goal is to create and maintain the Internet's most comprehensive site addressing issues for adopted children of color, offering informative articles on related topics as well as profiles of members and their families, links to other Internet resources, and a book reference guide with a searchable database. It publishes *Pact Press* periodically, and the site provides reprints of past *Pact Press* issues, as well as opportunities to interact with all parties involved in the adoption process, in cluding to ask questions of birth parents, adopted people, adoptive parents, and adoption professionals.

A Place for Us
PO Box 357, Gardena, CA   90248
e-mail: aplaceforusnational@yahoo.com
Web site: www.aplaceforusnational.com

A Place for Us offers support to multiracial families, individuals, and transracial adoption families. As an educational and advocacy group, this organization offers counseling to multiracial families and seeks to educate individuals and other organizations about multiracial issues. The founders of the organization have published a book titled *Life Through the Eyes of an Interracial Couple*, which is available on their Web site.

Project Race: Reclassify All Children Equally
PO Box 2366, Los Banos, CA   93635
fax: (209) 826-2510
e-mail: projrace@aol.com
Web site: www.projectrace.com

Project RACE is an advocacy organization for multiracial children and adults. It lobbies for multiracial interests in education, community awareness, and legislation. In particular, the organization advocates for a multiracial classification on all school, employment, state, federal, local, census, and medical forms requiring racial data. The Project RACE Web site features news items and links and provides information on multiracial advocacy volunteer opportunities for adults and teens.

Swirl, Inc.
244 Fifth Ave., Suite J230, New York, NY   10001-7604
(212) 561-1773
Web site: www.swirlinc.org

Swirl, Inc. is an antiracism grassroots organization that serves the mixed-heritage community and aims to develop a national consciousness around mixed-heritage issues to empower members to organize and take action toward progressive social change. Swirl has active chapters in New York City, Boston, and the Bay Area, with each chapter holding approximately two to six events per month. Swirl activities may include monthly dine-outs, book clubs, film screenings, discussions and panels, museum outings, family events, volunteer activities, and advocacy opportunities. The Swirl Web site maintains a regularly updated list of issues and events in which interested multiracial individuals can get involved.

For Further Research

Books

Lori Andrews, *Black Power, White Blood: The Life and Times of Johnny Spain*. New York: Pantheon, 1996.

Milton Barron, *The Blending American: Patterns of Intermarriage*. Chicago: Quadrangle, 1972.

Emily Bernard, ed., *Some of My Best Friends*. New York: Amistad, 2004.

J.R. Berzon, *Neither Black nor White: The Mulatto Character in American Fiction*. New York: New York University Press, 1978.

Janet Bode, *Different Worlds: Interracial and Cross-Cultural Dating*. New York: Franklin Watts, 1989.

Jane Ayers Chiong, *Racial Categorization of Multiracial Children in Schools*. Westport, CT: Bergin & Garvey, 1998.

Ellis Cose, *Color-Blind: Seeing Beyond Race in a Race-Obsessed World*. New York: HarperCollins, 1998.

Joel Crohn, *Mixed Matches: How to Create Successful Interracial, Interethnic and Interfaith Relationships*. New York: Fawcett, 1995.

Heather Dalmadge, *Tripping on the Color Line: Black-White Multiracial Families in a Racially Divided World*. Piscataway, NJ: Rutgers University Press, 2000.

G. Reginald Daniel, *More than Black? Multiracial Identity and the New Racial Order*. Philadelphia: Temple University Press. 2001.

Lise Funderburg, ed., *Black, White, Other: Biracial Americans Talk About Race*. New York: William Morrow, 1994.

Pearl Fuyo Gaskins, ed., *What Are You?* New York: Henry Holt, 1999.

Kathlyn Gay, *The Rainbow Effect: Interracial Families*. New York: Franklin Watts, 1987.

Jessie Carroll Grearson and Lauren B. Smith, eds., *Swaying: Essays on Intercultural Love*. Iowa City: University of Iowa Press, 1995.

Kimberly Hohman, *The Colors of Love: The Black Person's Guide to Interracial Relationships*. Chicago: Lawrence Hill, 2002.

Iris Jacob, ed., *My Sisters' Voices*. New York: Henry Holt, 2002.

Randall Kennedy, *Interracial Intimacies*. New York: Pantheon, 2003.

Jane Lazarre, *Beyond the Whiteness of Whiteness: Memoir of a White Mother of Black Sons*. Durham, NC: Duke University Press, 1996.

Karen Ma, *The Modern Madame Butterfly: Fantasy and Reality in Japanese Cross-Cultural Relationships*. North Clarendon, VT: Charles E. Tuttle, 1996.

Mark Mathabane and Gail Mathabane, *Love in Black and White: The Triumph of Love over Prejudice and Taboo*. New York: HarperCollins, 1992.

James McBride, *The Color of Water: A Black Man's Tribute to His White Mother*. New York: Riverhead, 1997.

David McCord and William Cleveland, *Black and Red: The Historical Meeting of Africans and Native Americans*. Atlanta: Dreamkeeper, 1990.

Edward Murgia, *Chicano Intermarriage*. San Antonio, TX: Trinity University Press, 1982.

Claudine Chiawei O'Hearn, ed., *Half + Half.* New York: Pantheon, 1998.

Ernest Porterfield, *Black and White Mixed Marriages.* Chicago: Nelson Hall, 1978.

Maria P.P. Root, *Love's Revolution: Interracial Marriage.* Philadelphia: Temple University Press, 2001.

Maria P.P. Root, ed., *The Multiracial Experience.* Thousand Oaks, CA: Sage, 1996.

Rita Simon, *Adoption Across Borders: Serving the Children in Transracial and Intercountry Adoptions.* Lanham, MD: Rowman and Littlefield, 2000.

Paul Spickard, *Mixed Blood: Intermarriage and Ethnic Identity in Twentieth-Century America.* Madison: University of Wisconsin Press, 1989.

Betty Lee Sung, *Chinese American Intermarriage.* New York: Center for Migration Studies, 1989.

Becky Thompson and Sangeeta Tyagi, eds., *Names We Call Home: Autobiography on Racial Identity.* New York: Routledge, 1996.

Rebecca Walker, *Black, White, and Jewish: Autobiography of a Shifting Self.* New York: Riverhead, 2000.

Naomi Zack, *American Mixed Race: The Culture of Microdiversity.* Lanham, MD: Rowman and Littlefield, 1995.

Periodicals

Jonathan Alter, "A Shabby Fiesta of Hypocrisy," *Newsweek,* November 2004.

Robert W. Butler, "Race in Your Face," *Kansas City (MO) Star,* February 2006.

Ayana Byrd, "Love Actually: The Man of Her Dreams Turned Out to Be Not Black, Not White, but 'Other,'" *Essence,* May 2005.

Rhonda Casey, "On a Cruise, a Painful Lesson," *Philadelphia Inquirer*, February 2006.

John Cha, "Mother Didn't Speak to Me for Five Years . . . ," *Audrey*, April/May 2005.

Gloria Cowan, "Interracial Interactions at Racially Diverse University Campuses," *Journal of Social Psychology*, February 2005.

Ebony, "The Last Taboo? Does Wave of Interracial Movies Signal a Real Change?" September 1991.

David J. Garrow, "'Oreo' Nation," *Washington Monthly*, March 2003.

Daisy Hernandez, "What's Love Got to Do with It?" *Colorlines*, Winter 2005.

Zondra Hughes, "Why Some Brothers Only Date Whites and 'Others,'" *Ebony*, January 2003.

Maureen Jenkins, "Mixed Feelings: Local Women Talk Interracial Dating as 'Something New' Lights Up the Big Screen," *Chicago Sun-Times*, February 3, 2006.

Lisa Jones and Hettie Jones, "Mama's White: Daughter of an Interracial Marriage and Her Mother Air Their Views," *Essence*, May 1994.

Vanessa Juarez, "Let's Talk About Race," *Newsweek*, February 2005.

David Knox, Marty E. Zusman, Carmen Buffington, and Gloria Hemphill, "Interracial Dating Attitudes Among College Students," *College Student Journal*, March 2000.

Elisabeth Lasch-Quinn, "How to Behave Sensitively: Prescriptions for Interracial Conduct from the 1960s to the 1990s," *Journal of Social History*, Winter 1999.

Lynn Norment, "Black Women White Men, White Women, Black Men: Interracial Relations," *Ebony*, November 1999.

Diane Parker, "Sanaa Lathan on Interracial Dating," *Salt Lake City Deseret News*, February 3, 2006.

Garry Pierre-Pierre, "The White Wife: Handling Reactions to Interracial Marriage," *Essence*, July 1998.

Laura B. Randolph, "Black Women—White Men: What's Goin' On?" *Ebony*, March 1989.

Michael D. Reiter, Jaimie M. Krause, and Amber Stirlen, "Intercouple Dating on a College Campus," *College Student Journal*, September 2005.

Shawn E. Rhea, "Black, White and Seeing Red All Over," *Colorlines*, Winter 2004.

Chris Rice, "Unfinished Business," *Christian Century*, August 9, 2005.

Steve Sailer, "Is Love Colorblind? Public Opinion About Interracial Marriage," *National Review*, July 14, 1997.

Allison Samuels, "She's Gotta Have Him," *Newsweek*, January 2006.

Kimberly J. Shinew, Troy D. Glover, and Diana C. Parry, "Leisure Spaces as Potential Sites for Interracial Interaction: Community Gardens in Urban Areas," *Journal of Leisure Research*, Third Quarter 2004.

Society for the Advancement of Education, "Interracial Marriages Common in Military," *USA Today* magazine, April 2004.

Carmen Van Kerckhove, "Media Betrays Society's Ambivalence Toward Interracial Relationships," *New/Demographic*, June 2005.

Rebecca Walker, "Black, White and Jewish," *Essence*, January 2001.

Mark Whatley, Julia N. Jahangardi, Rashonda Ross, and David Knox, "College Student Attitudes Toward Transracial Adoption," *College Student Journal*, September 2003.

Joe Wilensky, "Relationships: What Factors Affect the Occurrence of Interracial and Interethnic Relationships Among Adolescents?" *Human Ecology*, March 2002.

Walter E. Williams, "Racial Healing Requires Truth About Interracial Crime," *Human Events*, September 17, 1999.

Index